FREE
TO
BELIEVE

Donna,
    Keep on leading
your way into freeing
your self and your soul
because both are
beautiful and wonderful.

            Mary Crist

FREE
TO
BELIEVE

LIBERATING IMAGES
OF GOD FOR WOMEN

MARY CRIST BROWN

The Pilgrim Press
Cleveland, Ohio

The Pilgrim Press, Cleveland, Ohio 44115
www.pilgrimpress.com
© 2000 by Mary Crist Brown

05 04 03 02 01 00   5 4 3 2 1

Library of Congress Cataloging-in-Publication Data
Brown, Mary Crist, 1955–.
    Free to believe / Mary Crist Brown.
      p. cm.
    Includes bibliographical references (p.).
    ISBN 0-8298-1394-2 (pbk. : alk. paper)
    1. Image of God. 2. Women—Religious life. 3. Christian
women—Religious life. 4. Self-perception in women—Religious
aspects. 5. Femininity of God. I. Title.

BL205 .B76 2000
231'.4—dc21

                              00-034346

To the many women who have inspired
and supported me in my journey to re-imagine my life

Contents

Introduction

Images of God have a powerful impact on the human psyche, particularly since we live in a world where there is an inter-relationship between self, religion, and culture. Both theology and psychology claim that no one in Western civilization is without an image of God. When we talk about God, we use a description that is a likeness or mental picture of who we understand God to be. We know that there is no single image to describe God totally because God is beyond human description. At the same time, we use language to attempt to communicate about our experience and understanding of God. These descriptions come from our human images of God and from our experience of God as creativity, mystery, and loving energy in the world.

Because God created us in God's image male and female, gender is one of the ways we use language to describe God. Since we live in a patriarchal culture where father is considered the head of the house and male is first-class and female is second-class, our psyches have incorporated these cultural beliefs into our images of God. Western culture functions by means of gender polarity where male is dominant and female is subordinate. As a part of culture, the church falls prey to gender polarity as well. God is he and not she.

Within the Judeo-Christian tradition, the predominant image for God is Father. The image of God as Father impacts our self-perceptions and development. For many women, the image of God as Father blocks both spiritual and emotional growth. As a pastoral counselor, I am concerned about what enables spiritual and emotional growth in people. As a female, I am particularly interested in what helps or hinders healthy self-development in females. Through my experience as a pastoral counselor, I recognize a connection between a person's image of God and ability to have healthy self-development.

In my counseling practice, I encounter women who feel frustrated by the traditional male images of the Judeo-Christian God. God as Father in a negative way can lead to feelings of hurt, guilt, shame, self-sacrifice, and devaluing in females. God as Father in a positive way conjures up images of protector and provider. My concern in this book is to explore the way God as Father can be harmful to female self-development when females are not aware of the powerful impact of God images on the human psyche and on self-development.

The traditional male images of God (Father, Son, Master, King, Lord, etc.) need liberating to provide images of God for females that support the unique emotional and spiritual needs of females. In our Western culture we have no female images of God equal to the male God images. Divine Feminine, Goddess, Gaia, and Sophia are not considered primary God images in our Western culture. They are secondary or second-class images.

Although there are positive images of females in the Bible, I did not begin to discover them until I was in seminary. In church school and church I heard mostly about negative female images for God. Eve, the woman who caused our expulsion from the Garden of Eden and is proof of female moral inferiority. The pagan fertility goddesses who were sinful and evil. Bathsheba, who through her beauty lured David into committing murder and is evidence of female seductiveness. Mary, the blessed mother of Jesus, who must never be thought of as God, yet must remain a virgin. Only on Mother's Day were females seen in a positive manner through platitudes that placed mothers on a pedestal.

The aim of liberating God images is to provide a way for females to discover and choose images of God that facilitate healthy female self-development. The aim is not to exclude or replace male images but to create a space to have both male and female God images. As human beings, we can never completely define God, yet we use language and images to talk about God. Because God transcends our human condition, our images and definitions of God are rooted in our human perceptions and interpretations of God. If God is beyond definition, why have we limited our images of God? Why are we not free to believe many images of God?

I am interested in this question because as both a pastor and a counselor, I know there is a direct connection between the images we use for God, self, culture, and family and how we understand our own self-image. For example, in the past male was strong and female was weak. Consequently, females grew up feeling inferior because that is how femaleness was defined. Females are born into a feminine wound of inferiority. Anne Wilson Schaef writes, "To be born female in this culture means that you are born 'tainted' . . . I am not implying that this must remain so. I do believe that we must know this and understand it as a given before it can be worked through."[1]

God as predominantly male images and negative or secondary female images can contribute to females feeling like second-class citizens. The purpose of liberating images of God is for females to work through the devaluing, "tainted" images that reside inside the self so that room can be made to explore new images of God and self.

This book focuses on re-imagining and re-imaging images of God and self rather than on recovering feminine biblical and nonbiblical images of God. Much has been written on the wealth of female God images that are available. More important to me is the process where a person learns to use her imagination. In her book *A God Who Looks Like Me*, Patricia Reilly writes, "The traditional images of Father and Son were so specific that I had no freedom for my own imaginings."[2] I believe there are many women who have never thought about or given themselves the opportunity to exercise their imaginations envisioning God as other than male.

I am interested in offering a process for females to re-imagine God. If I can imagine, then I have the ability to create space to discover and change myself within the limits of my humanness. I can use old images and create new images that fit my unique self and needs.

The book explores, first, the interrelationship of self-image and God image. Next are stories of various women struggling with issues of inequality, self-sacrifice and guilt, self-denial and anger, and physical and sexual abuse. All of these stories highlight the connection between self-image and God image and suggest ways for liberating images of God. The stories are composite sketches compiled from several women who had similar experiences. The names and identifying characteristics of the women are changed to protect their confidentiality. Finally, the book offers a method that allows for various ways for females to re-image God.

Free to Believe: Liberating Images of God for Women is written for females of all ages and cultural/religious diversity. The common denominator is the struggle to deal with the impact of male God images and to learn ways to re-image God. Because Western culture is predominantly Judeo-Christian in its religious heritage, the images of God explored are from this tradition, although not limited to it. The book can be read by churchgoers and non-churchgoers. In particular, this book will appeal to women who are searching for new or different images of God other than the traditional ones. The book is for women who wish to deal with and understand the interrelationship of self-image and God images.

1

Self-Image and God Image

When I was six years old, God was love to me. I got confused at church because most of the time God was called Father. Did this mean that my human father was God? I did not experience my father that way. And why, if God was Father, was God never called Mother? I had both a mother and a father. Although I did not understand intellectually that there was a preference given to males in church and society, I could feel the disparity at age six.

Reluctantly, I adopted the language of the church. As I grew older, I realized that God is beyond our human descriptions and definitions. I thought of God as Love, Mystery, Justice, Peace, Creator, Redeemer, and Sustainer, yet there still lived inside me the notion that the true definition for God was Father. The Lord's Prayer begins, "Our Father, who art in heaven . . ." This is a foundational prayer we learn as children and recite often in church.

My first awakening to the power of gendered God images came through my work as a chaplain with emotionally troubled boys, ages ten through sixteen. When acting out the parable of the lost son, a colleague and I asked the boys to finish the story at the point that the son returns home to the father. In the parable, the father embraces the prodigal son and even celebrates his return with a party. That was not the ending the boys created. Instead, when they returned home, the father either slammed the door in the son's face or violently beat the son.

The boys' experience of neglect and abuse from their earthly fathers made them wary of believing that God as Father could be loving and just. Because the predominant image of God was that of Father, the troubled boys had difficulty in finding a place to connect with God. Maybe if God were defined as Mother or Sister or Compassionate and Forgiving Being or any of a number of other images, the boys might have had an easier time connecting with God. It was clear to me that they experienced God the Father as judgmental and abusive, and I pondered the impact of God images on the self.

God created human beings to be object seeking. We require relationships for our growth. In psychological language an object is a significant person with whom you have a relationship. We are able to relate to each other because of the significant relationships in our lives that begin in infancy. An infant takes inside herself or himself images of the parents and of significant people. These snapshots create internal images of significant people that keep them alive for the infant. Because the infant is dependent on the parent, the infant experiences anxiety when the parent is out of sight. The snapshots of parenting figures calm the infant by lessening anxiety when the parent is out of sight.

Like snapshots, these images may or may not be in focus, but the infant believes the internal images to be clear pictures of the objects. In this way we can understand how distortions of parents and others can occur. The infant begins to create a photo album of mother, father, brother, sister, and other significant people. Attached to these snapshots are clusters of feelings—positive, negative, and neutral. These snapshots enable us starting in infancy to recognize people to whom we relate.

These snapshots are called object representations, which are influenced by family, culture, religion, and other elements. The primary internal object representations come from the main caregiver, usually the mother with help from the father. When an infant is born, a preset developmental process leads the self to seek and relate with external objects such as the parents. Psychic structure is built through the self's experience with the external objects and with the external environment. An internal system of snapshots develops. This photo album relates to itself in an ongoing process whereby it adds, subtracts, and edits its object representations.

As the infant grows and develops, the view of the external object changes so that the infant internalizes a new version of the object. Inside the photo album are snapshots representing, remembering, and fantasizing about both good and bad objects. The good object representations are available to relate with other good objects and represent feelings of satisfaction and the desire for growth and positive interaction. Good object representations lead to developing positive self-esteem. The bad objects represent feelings of abandonment, rejection, neglect, despair, self-hatred, and devaluing, and they pool together to form snapshots that are out of focus yet often very present in controlling the infant's life. These bad object representations lead to demeaning and devaluing images and feelings of the self, which create low self-esteem.

Because even the good enough parent is frustrating and rejecting at times, the infant splits off and represses intolerable feelings of anxiety and abandonment. To hold on to the good image of the parent, the infant takes inside the self and splits off and represses the rejecting or threatening image of the parent. The task of life is to achieve full object constancy where there is the capacity to tolerate both frustration and satisfaction from object relations.

To achieve object constancy, a person must be capable of tolerating the unwelcome presence of repressed and split-off aspects and feelings of the self. Then the self must use the imagination to modify and integrate these object relations into a coherent image of the self. In achieving object constancy as human beings, we learn to validate and accept what is positive about ourselves, identify and accept our limitations, and re-image the false negative self-images.

Each person we meet will activate different aspects of our good object relations and our split-off and repressed object relations. When we meet a new person, we will expect the new relationship to be like those known in the past, primarily from external object relations with the parent(s). We have a tendency to seek likeness even where there is difference. Someone who is unaware of this process can become easily disappointed when the new relationship turns out to be more different from what was initially thought.

Whenever disharmony with original object representations occurs, the person experiences internal conflict within the photo album. The disharmony can be acknowledged and integrated through re-imaging, or it can be pushed back into the unconscious again. Encountering difference and disappointment is an opportunity to rearrange and/or re-image the self's photo album.

In general, human beings resist change and the loss that accompanies even positive change.[1] Through resistance, persons repress painful feelings and images and keep such feelings and images in the unconscious. We have a tendency to keep our original bonds with our early object relations, usually the mother and/or father, even though re-imaging might lead to healthier relating.

One great fear is who or what will replace them if the internal parents are deactivated.[2] The threat of changing a special, past image of the self is resisted particularly when conflictual material, guilty wishes, unacceptable feelings, or anxiety-ridden memories emerge.

In all of our photo albums are pictures of the family, pictures of cultural messages, and photos from our religious traditions. Throughout our lives, our photo albums have the capacity to be in an ongoing process of integration and editing. The photo albums may be put up on a shelf and forgotten, or selected photos may be lost. These forgotten, ignored, and lost photos continue to influence us whether or not we are aware of them. Our photo albums tell us what to feel about ourselves and about others.

For the emotionally troubled boys I worked with, their photo albums contained photos of abusive fathers. My guess is that they were in-focus pictures. However, because their photo albums contained few, if any, photos of nurturing fathers, they were left with a distorted understanding of father. This in turn meant that they regarded God as Father as abusive.

Symbols and images that we use through language function in a similar manner to our internal object representations, except that they are external. In fact, the capacity for object relating leads to the capacity for creating symbols. Object representations are created from our human relationships, and symbols are created from our external relationships. Images of God are like an external photo album of what human beings think and feel about God.

Psychiatrist Ana-Maria Rizzuto theorizes that psychologically each person's image of God is created out of facts and fantasies of wishes, hopes, fears, powerful mysteries, and images of parents and other significant people.[3] Not only the parent of real life but the wished-for parent and feared parent of the imagination appear as equal contributors to the created image of God.[4] Images of God are created out of an ongoing interplay between external and internal representations of self, others, and God.

As human beings, we create object representations of the internal self process and representations of our experience with the external world. These representations are the symbols and images we create through religion, art, and culture. Our internal and external worlds do not remain separated. In an intermediate area of experience that psychiatrist Donald Winnicott called transitional space, the internal and external representations meet.[5] This transitional space offers a neutral place for a creative conversation between differing personal, religious, and cultural understandings of self and God. In this space God images are created and re-created throughout life.

While we are growing up, we hear people talk about God. There are official representations of God in pastors, priests, and rabbis, among others. They speak to the child about special buildings as "God's house." People talk about God in a respectful and believing way. Adults may tell the child that God will "punish him," "bless him," or "love him." The child senses that God is powerful, is everywhere, and rules everything. The closest parallel to the child's experience of God is the experience of the parents. The growing child will utilize the most significant parent available to create his or her God representation.[6]

Our images of God develop just as we develop. By the age of two and a half, a child cognitively understands that things are made by people. When the two-and-a-half-year-old finally asks, "Who made God?" she will not be able to comprehend that nobody made God. This answer usually frustrates the child's knowledge that somebody makes things but conveys the sense to the child that God is not ordinary. By age three, the child wants to know whether God has the same body parts as human beings do and whether God lives in a house with a television, computer, telephone, and more. By age five, the child wants to know whether God is a man or a woman and where God lives.[7]

By age six, the child understands God as Creator of the world, of animals, of beautiful things. The child develops a feeling relationship with God, making prayer important to him or her. For me at age six, God was the feeling of love. It can be interesting to think back to age six or so and try to recapture your feelings about God. Doing this will help you to realize some of your basic feelings about God. Whether God is loving or judgmental, abusive or protective, is determined to a large extent by early feelings toward parents mixed with early experiences of God.

The feeling relationship with God is very much impacted by the child's experience with her or his parents, religious community, and culture. The child may deal with the realization of having destructive feelings using the cultural image of the devil. Images of the devil and monsters are used as well to handle the child's anxiety that parents and other adults could easily destroy the child. This is an attempt to contain these destructive feelings and fears.[8] In object relations language this is called splitting. The object representation, or snapshot, is split into good and bad images to lessen the child's anxiety by protecting the good aspects of the internal image. No parent is totally good.

Primarily, the image of the devil is male. There is no female image of the devil. This seems to parallel the reality of male dominance in Western culture. The destructiveness and fear of the mother are absorbed culturally by witches.[9] The problem for females is that witches are earthly and not heavenly. Destructive feelings toward females remain in the human realm; in other words, the witch becomes "the bitch." Destructive feelings toward males are placed in the devil or God, both in the supranatural realm, which keeps these feelings from being destructively placed on human males. Human females bear the brunt of destructive feelings.

At this age, the child may split the positive feelings into heroes and superheroes. Often cartoon characters become important, and the child wants to own Ninja Turtles, X-Men, Star Wars characters, and on and on. If you have a female child who wants a superhero different from Barbie or an American Girl doll, you know it is difficult to find these toys, although many of the cartoons now have female superheroes. The X-Men have Storm and Rogue, but it is rare to find one of them to purchase. I searched high and low throughout Atlanta before I found Catwoman. There are female Power Rangers, but all of the Power Rangers are androgynous looking. Female children need to experience female heroes and superheroes. A powerful cultural message is being delivered when all heroes and super-heroes are male.

As the child grows and develops, the child naturally experiences disappointments and disillusionments with the parent(s). God images can provide the child with people who truly appreciate her or him. Heaven becomes a place where everything is wonderful and where Someone is more powerful than the parents. As the child begins to separate from parents and develop a sense of self, the child usually will experience loneliness. God at this point can be a companion for the child, helping to lessen the loneliness.[10]

Children around age ten may experience "existential loneliness." They become aware that their parents have a partner, but they do not. Having friends and companions becomes important. God may become Someone who listens, understands, and befriends them. However, if at this point the child's representation of God is negative and/or frightening, the child may not be able to make positive use of the God image to assuage loneliness. The negative God image can contribute to feeling even lonelier.

During early adolescence, the child developmentally has the capacity for abstract thinking and can think of God conceptually beyond concrete descriptions. The adolescent can begin to construct philosophical and theological arguments about God. During late adolescence, he or she has a need to integrate a growing sense of self with a God image.[11] For example, how does my image of God help or hinder with decisions about life and self—vocation, relationships, and culture? During this time, there is the possibility of encountering new God images and reshuffling the self-image with the new and old God images. The adolescent often explores and tests God images as he or she does everything else.

If the image of God is not revised as a child develops, that image will eventually become obsolete, irrelevant, contrary to life experience, or dangerous to healthy development. A child may choose to bury the God image and/or discard religion as useful.[12] This happens particularly if the adolescent is not encouraged and/or allowed to explore and test personal beliefs about God. One can go throughout life with a stagnant image of God that comes from an early stage of development that is not helpful for living adult life. If images of God are explored, the adolescent has the opportunity to discover a helpful adult image of God. Adolescents can learn that their image of God grows and changes as they grow.

Development does not end with adolescence. We continue to develop until we die. Psychoanalyst Erik Erikson developed eight stages of the human life cycle. His stages are made up of both the positive and the negative feelings a person can experience at each stage. There are times when we revisit different stages as we continue to move forward into the next stage. It is often true that the image of God and feelings about God are related to how well we have negotiated each of these stages.

These stages are trust/mistrust (infancy), autonomy/shame and doubt (early childhood), initiative/guilt (play age), industry/inferiority (school age), identity/identity confusion (adolescence), intimacy/isolation (young adulthood), generativity/stagnation (adulthood), and integrity/despair (mature adulthood). We continue to have opportunities to make changes in our self object representations and in our God images.

We have the ongoing chance to re-image God in a way that will be constructive for living. Some adolescents may find God wanting and so drop the image of God. Others may keep a restrictive and/or judgmental image of God. The hope is that we find a God image compatible with our beliefs and self-development. God images modulate feelings of children and perceived failures of parents. Helpful God images lead to a sense of communion with ourselves and with the Sacred. We then know and trust that we are connected to something greater than ourselves.

From Erikson's stages we know that feelings of trust/mistrust and shame and guilt are related to our self-development and God images. These feelings influence our self-worth and self-esteem. Our level of self-understanding and self-esteem influences our definition of God, and our definition of God affects our selves. "Esteem" comes from the same root word as "estimate," so self-esteem is the genuine expression of a person's thoughts and feelings about self that occurs in an ongoing evaluation/estimation process. Foundational self-esteem refers to a child's feeling genuinely loved and accepted. Secondary self-esteem is achieved through positive relationships and the reworking of early negative feelings, thoughts, and self-images. The more self-esteem a person has, the more she or he is able to be open to a diversity of images of God, self, and world.

Openness to a diversity of images is important because human beings use images of God to bolster positive self-esteem and/or to devalue self-esteem, depending on the God image and how it is used. Human beings use images of God to place good and bad feelings, valued and dangerous feelings, about self and others. If the traditional, cultural symbols of God are harmonious with a person's self-representation, then these images enable healthy self-development and self-esteem. If the images of God conflict with self-representations, then these images can lead to unhealthy self-development and negative self-esteem.

Human beings place into God images both the need for idealizing (placing above the self as if on a pedestal) and the need for demeaning (placing lower than the self, as in being a second-class citizen). This can be a positive psychological function of God images. However, a problem is created because in our culture we do not have equal female God images with our male God images. For example, anger and disappointment at human males can be given to God as Father; the symbol of God as Father contains these feelings for us.

It is helpful and sometimes safer to be angry with God rather than with our human fathers or other significant males.

Because there is not a comparable female symbol of God with the symbol of God as Father, there is no symbol on which females and males can place feelings of anger, rage, and disappointment toward females. Consequently, these feelings are placed/projected into females (often mother, wife, sister, or daughter) rather than into a symbol.

Instead of having a Divine Feminine symbol, females must become all-giving and self-sacrificing or all-powerful as human beings. The feminine images of God are either glorified or devalued, neither of which encourages a healthy view of the female self. Females become the all-powerful mother/woman or the all-giving mother/woman, both of which are feared or revered and neither of which allows a female to be her true self. It is my belief that equal female God images would help to eliminate this dichotomy and would work to heal many female wounds.

The only biblical scripture that specifically describes the "image of God" is Genesis 1:27: "So God created humankind in his image, in the image of God he created them; male and female he created them." God created them, not him. In Genesis 1:27, the structure of the Hebrew language does not place male over female but signifies a mutual relationship between male and female, equally being made in the image of God. A scholar of the Hebrew Scriptures, Phyllis Trible, writes, "Created simultaneously, male and female are not superior and subordinate. Neither has power over the other; in fact, both are given equal power."[13]

Genesis 2:7–24 describes the creation of Adam. Here, according to Trible, the Hebrew word Adam means "earth creature," being both and neither male nor female.[14] Only when the earth creature becomes lonely does God create a companion by introducing sexual differences. It is God who creates Adam and Eve out of the earth creature, not Adam who creates Eve. The relationship between the two earth creatures is as helper, which means a beneficial relationship between two parties where one helps the other. This is in the tradition of God being called a helper of Israel. There is no sense of the helper being inferior or subordinate; the helper is a partner.[15]

Unfortunately, this description of humanity as being created in the image of God, male and female, has been interpreted traditionally in a hierarchical manner placing male over female. When I went to seminary in the late 1970s, inclusive language was a major issue. The opposition to using inclusive language argued that since God created "man" in "his" own image and "man" was understood to be generic, there was no need for the inclusion of feminine descriptions.

The proponents of inclusive language argued that the language we use significantly defines our understanding of reality; if male language is used, that is reality. The question that always nagged at me was this: If equality already exists with our generic, universal understanding of man, why was there so much opposition to expanding our description of God to include the feminine? My conclusion was that there is power in language to name and to define reality; thus, inclusive language would upset the power imbalance between males and females. Gender really was a political issue and continues to be an issue.

My firsthand experience of gender as a major issue occurred when I went to work as an associate pastor in a church that had never before had an ordained female pastor. My femaleness had both positive and negative impacts. Many members felt fine about my doing the traditional female tasks of Christian education and youth ministry but cringed at the idea of my preaching, baptizing, and serving communion. The sacraments were considered male tasks. When one of my ordained married female colleagues got pregnant, her congregation went into an uproar over whether she should serve communion. We surmised that the dissension had to do with her having sex to get pregnant. Sex and the sacraments were to remain separate from each other rather than a part of life and marriage.

One of my positive experiences stemmed from the senior pastor's insistence on the staff's using inclusive language in the worship service, and whenever possible, the senior pastor made sure that both a male and a female were leading worship and performing the sacraments. Over the course of several years, a number of members, mostly female, told me that the use of inclusive language and my female presence were having a significant impact on their understanding of God as including females. Whenever I was out of town, they could feel a difference in the worship service. The presence of a male and a female in worship modeled for the worshipers the image of God as male and female.

Some people argue now that we no longer need inclusive language or re-imaging because we live in a post–women's liberation age. Although the Equal Rights Amendment failed, they contend that women have equal rights. This argument does not take into account that more than five thousand years of patriarchy continue to impact our psyches, religion, and culture.

One day Jane came home from the first grade with severe frustration. I am close friends with Jane's mother, and Jane and I are close. She told me about there being a girls' club and a boys' club in her classroom. That arrangement seemed typical for first graders. The problem was that in the girls' club the girls could draw pictures only of ballerinas and pretty ladies. The girls made the rule, which could not be broken. In the boys' club the youngsters could draw pictures of whatever they wanted; there were no restrictions. Jane felt torn because she wanted to be with her female peers but did not want to be restricted in her drawing. Since there was no flexibility in the girls' club, she joined the boys' club, which was willing to accept her.

I wailed inside at the reality of a creative six-year-old girl child having to deal with the pain of the limitations that patriarchy has placed on females and trying to know how to relate to other girls who were not aware that there was a limitation in drawing pictures only of ballerinas. From early in her life, Jane was exposed to a multiplicity of God images, both traditional and nontraditional. At age three her image of God was of a goddess with long red hair. I happen to have red hair so I could not help feeling some pride in her modeling her image of God after me. Young children will image God after significant people in their lives.

Now at age twelve, Jane images God as "him," "he," and "Father." One could say that she is just growing up. Or one could say that the older she gets, the more she is influenced by culture and a patriarchal church, and the more she limits her thoughts, feelings, and imaginings about God so that she will fit in and will conform to cultural expectations of who females are meant to be. Her older brother has more freedom to conceptualize God as Father and Mother than Jane does. All of this is despite the fact that Jane has a mother who uses inclusive language to describe God in a multitude of inclusive ways.

God as male is embedded in the conscious and unconscious belief structures, whether or not one thinks of God as male. When I asked Jane about why she called God "he," she said it was just easier that way. She knew that God was male and female, but the people at church used male God images most of the time. Jane, who has divorced parents, goes to two very different Baptist churches. Her father's church is traditional in its use of God images. Her mother's church uses inclusive language. Most of the time she goes to her father's church, because she spends her weekends with him.

On occasion Jane goes to her mother's church. I was relieved a bit when at a church retreat that was encouraging the exploration of a variety of images of God, Jane described God as the Colorful. She said, "I believe that God is a man and a woman and that we all have different colors inside us. When we die and go to heaven, we make God colorful." Why do too many females limit their thoughts, feelings, and imaginings?

Jane has the opportunity to re-image God because her family and her mother's church encourage her to explore her images of God. At the church retreat, time and space were provided for her to come up with her own image of God. Since the theme of the retreat was gaining some understanding of the one hundred different names for Allah, there was plenty of room to diverge from tradition and to use one's imagination. No one was going to judge another person's God image. We were learning about Allah because one of the church members was living in Morocco and participating in a Christian-Muslim dialogue.

Space and the use of imagination are required for re-imaging God. As a person trained in psychology, I know that people fear change. We human beings like to conform and to repeat the past. We like to stick with the old and acceptable images, whether these pictures work for us or not. Our personal snapshots resist rearranging. How much power these past images have determines how much freedom we have to liberate God images through re-imagining.

At the same time, as spiritual people we are called by God to newness. In the Christian tradition, God creates a new covenant (Jer. 31:31), and God through Jesus Christ offers us a new creation (2 Cor. 5:17). I believe that God's vision attempts to lure humanity to change through introducing newness into set belief structures. God attempts to encourage people through the pull of God's love to make choices that open the door to positive and constructive changes leading to a greater ability to love and relate with each other.

As a pastoral counselor, I am concerned with the capacity of a person's soul to have options for self-transcendence. I believe self-transcendence is the person's ability to use creativity and imagination to move from past beliefs into future beliefs. I believe human beings have the capacity to rearrange their photo albums and to add new photos. The following chapters are illustrations of various women's struggles to take devaluing self-images and cultural images and to re-image self-images and God images in a way that allowed them to have a healthier relationship with themselves, others, and God.

2

The God I Worship Is Not Fair to Me

May asked me, "Do you believe God thinks females are equal to males?" When I asked her what she thought, her answer was no. I appreciated her honesty but felt sad that she did not believe that God thought she was equal to males. May grew up in a conservative home with a father who believed in the traditional gender roles.

In many ways May believed her father was God. He was head of the household. Her mother was a traditional homemaker who spent her time rearing her children and tending the home. The family went to a church run by the men. There were no female elders or deacons. Women were there to serve the men. Everyone talked about God solely in male images. May told me, "I grew up believing in 1 Timothy 2:11–14." This piece of scripture reads, "Let a woman learn in silence with full submission. I permit no woman to teach or to have authority over a man; she is to keep silent. For Adam was formed first, then Eve; and Adam was not deceived, but the woman was deceived and became a transgressor."

May experienced an ongoing conflict between the values with which she was raised, telling her to revere and respect her father and males more than females, and the reality of who her father was. As an adult, she recognized that although her father was an elder in the church, he drank too much alcohol and had multiple affairs. She described her mother as sweet, gentle, and forgiving to a fault. It was ironic to her that women were the "transgressors"; in her experience men transgressed more than women did.

Following her cultural programming, May married. Her husband turned out to drink too much and to have affairs. Unlike her mother, May decided to divorce her husband. After her divorce, May put herself through school and landed a good job. She is a successful professional woman now, but she still struggles with believing she has a right to be as worthy as her father and equal with her male work peers. May came to therapy because she was tired of having low self-esteem. She was tired of feeling guilty anytime she did not submit.

Not all of us grew up in such extreme circumstances, yet all of us are impacted by gender polarity. Gender polarity is the traditional cultural system in Western civilization in which male is dominant over female and male identity is defined in opposition to female identity. An example of gender polarity is the traditional view that maleness equals strength; thus, femaleness equals weakness. Males are dominant and females are submissive.

I grew up in a more moderate household; nevertheless, my parents modeled gender polarity in that my father worked and my mother was a homemaker. My brothers and I shared the chores, whether that was dishwashing or grass cutting. My father taught me how to change the oil and tires of a car. I learned from him how to paint and hammer and do other "handyman" chores. Wherever I work, I end up being the person who oversees the facilities. I am glad my father taught me these useful things that traditionally fall in the male realm.

The Presbyterian church I attended used predominantly male images for God. However, it began to elect female elders and deacons when I was in high school. My mother was one of the first female elders. By the time I was sixteen, she went to work as a school nurse. I was proud of her for those accomplishments.

I will be forever grateful to the pastor of my home church. When I was seventeen, I told him that I was interested in following a Christian vocation such as Christian education. suggested that I go into the ministry instead. It was 1972, and I had never seen a female minister. He explained to me that the church had begun ordaining females to the ministry. If I wanted to have a vote on the issues facing the church, I needed to be ordained. He also indicated that since I was very bright, why not go to the top?

With his encouragement I pursued ordination. I am not sure I would have known to pursue ordination if he had not suggested it. Not many pastors in the 1970s would have encouraged females to go to seminary. Only 15 percent of my seminary class were female. Today more than 50 percent of seminary classes are female, yet many of the same issues of inequality still exist. Why is there inequality for females in church and society?

Since our Western culture is predominantly Judeo-Christian, one way to understand the roots of gender polarity is to understand how the Bible and Judeo-Christian tradition image females. The Judeo-Christian religion is patriarchal, meaning "father-rule." It sets up a hierarchy of God-male-female. As theologian Rosemary Radford Ruether writes, "Women no longer stand in direct relation to God; they are connected to God secondarily, through the male."[1]

Religious membership was open only to men. The priesthood was restricted to men. Women could not study the Scriptures. Women could participate in religious services but with many restrictions. If a woman was ritually unclean due to menstruation or recent childbirth, she was restricted. Women were kept separate from men during the service.

Even in today's Orthodox Jewish service a veil separates male from female. Men were cautioned about speaking to women in public. The fear was that a woman could seduce and corrupt a man. Religious writer Barbara MacHaffie comments, "The rabbinic religion regards women as socially and religiously inferior to men and sometimes even expresses contempt for them."[2]

Women occupied a dependent and subordinate position. A female lived under the rule of her father. At marriage, the woman passed from the authority of the father to the authority of the husband. In ancient Israel, a woman was expected to marry and produce children. MacHaffie says, "Her fulfillment was found in serving her husband and particularly in supplying him with many sons."[3] Respect was given to the role of mother.

Women never lost their dependent status. If a woman was widowed, she turned to her sons for her care. Because economic benefits came from husbands and sons, it was important to bear sons. Females were required to be virgins before marriage, but males were not. A husband could divorce his wife, but a wife could not divorce her husband. Divorce led to dispossession for the female.

If a man and a woman were caught in adultery, the penalty was death for both of them. Generally, though, the woman was caught when she became pregnant. A wife who committed adultery was regarded as deceitful, but there was no penalty for a husband who engaged in sexual relations with a single woman outside marriage.[4]

In the Christian Scriptures with Jesus placing value on faith, not gender, there is some hope for female equality. Jesus never treated a woman as inferior. Jesus let unclean women touch him (Luke 8:40–56) and permitted women to speak to him in public (John 4:1–42). With the story of Mary and Martha (Luke 10:38–42) Jesus placed value on teaching women the Scriptures. There were female disciples (Matt. 27:55–56; Mark 15:40–41; Luke 8:1–3). After his resurrection, Jesus Christ first appeared to women.

Women were included as full members of the Christian community. Women led house churches, spread Christianity through missionary work, and held positions of leadership. So what happened to the movement for equality started by Jesus that was based on faith and not gender? Unfortunately, religion and culture influence faith. The egalitarian strand of Christianity was overcome by the antifemale, patriarchal strand that was institutionalized in 312 c.e. when Christianity became the official Roman religion. MacHaffie writes, "The Jewish male of Paul's day was expected to thank God daily that he was not a Gentile, a slave, or a woman."[5]

In its beginning, the early church was small and under persecution. To fit in and survive, the church adopted the traditional cultural and religious values. It inherited the institutional structure of the Jewish synagogue and the customs and prejudices related to the status of women. The majority of passages in the Christian Scriptures that place women in submissive positions were written between 80 and 125 c.e. So the dominant image of woman became submissive wife and mother. Although Jesus did not devalue women, the church succumbed to subordinating them.

Throughout the years, the devaluing of women was supported and at times intensified. Augustine believed that although women were equal in Christ's baptism, women could be easily overcome by physical passion because their spirits and minds were weak. Women were responsible for sin in the world and were inferior. Aquinas believed that women were created subordinate and inferior to men with less intellectual ability to make moral decisions. Women were "defective" human beings.

During the Protestant Reformation, a few steps forward were made for women in the theologies of Luther and Calvin. Both Calvin and Luther objected to the view of women as the despised sex or as evil. Men and women had the same potential for sin and for redemption. However, men and women were called to different vocations. The woman's place was in the home caring for children and accepting the rule of men. A woman could disobey her husband if her life was in danger or if obeying him would lead her to disobey God. Both Calvin and Luther called for general education of girls and boys.

With the colonization of America and the influence of the Puritans came a backward shift for women. Women were to be kept under control and were to be submissive and obedient. By the mid-nineteenth century, women were still to be submissive and were seen as morally pure and pious. Power and happiness for women were at home as wife and mother. Women were prone to sin, like Eve, so a split occurred where women were either superior as paragons of virtue and piety or inferior as temptresses. It is easy to see many of the roots of our current struggles with women's equality in religion, with sexual mores, and with economic issues for women.

Recently, my parents celebrated their fiftieth wedding anniversary. My brother purchased a 1949 popular women's magazine as a gift for my mother. Looking through the magazine, we were appalled by its focus and message. The articles were about cooking, raising children, working with the latest appliances, and learning how to take care of "your man." In one article a woman was struggling with whether to continue her education or do the sensible thing and settle down with a husband; the writer advised her to give up school and embrace the pleasures of married life. Although I knew that gender roles were very defined in the 1940s and 1950s, it was shocking to see how blatant they were. They were not that far from ancient Israel's view of women.

Our understanding of what it means to be male and female comes from our religious, cultural, and family beliefs and roles. These images become embedded in our psyches and are a part of our photo albums. To change these images and roles, there has to be a change in religious and cultural beliefs as well as a change in the inferior and superior images embedded in our psyches.

Theologian Bernard Meland believes that we are impacted by what he calls a cultural orbit of meaning. That is, a particular cultural history creates a characteristic mind-set that influences our psyches. The orbit of meaning gives structure and direction to our psyches and can be altered only if we pay attention to it and work on changing it.[6] In the case of Western civilization our orbit of meaning is patriarchal and redemptive.

In the midst of the set patriarchal orbit of meaning is the reality of God's redemptive presence. Redemption means being open to change through God's many possibilities. God is present within our cultural orbit of meaning calling us to newness. Although we cannot escape our orbits of meaning, we can be open to God's redemptive presence calling us to be new creations. Society is not set but is in the process of developing and changing over time, just as human beings grow and change. To make the changes happen, we have to rely on God's power and presence and on our own ability to become aware of our orbits of meaning and how we want to change them.

Under a patriarchal orbit of meaning, there are defined gender roles and defined ways of relating—God, male, female, in that order. Psychoanalyst Doris Bernstein notes, "Gender pervades every aspect of mental functioning." Every society provides identity models (orbits of meaning) that act as guides for how to be male and female. Currently, we are confronting a cultural upheaval in what it means to be male and female. The old identity models are no longer working. The model of femininity that was presented to us as children does not fit our current lives.[7]

Since our identity models are in flux, it seems important to me that we understand how these models are changing and search for models that can lead to healthier ways of relating as male and female. As we know, gender polarity is established under patriarchy. Gender polarity is the dominant-subordinate structure that places male over female; we cannot relate in a mutual way because mutuality does not exist structurally. Under gender polarity, relating occurs through one person being up and the other person being down. Subject (dominant person) relates to object (subordinate person).

When we are subjects, we are our own selves without the need to devalue or idolize the other person for us to feel good and powerful. Mutual relating happens when subject relates to subject. Psychoanalyst Jessica Benjamin believes that for healthy growth, human beings need mutual recognition. In mutual recognition subject relates to subject. I have my identity; you have your identity. We relate when I am able to see who you are and listen to you (recognize you). It means recognizing and valuing the other person's feelings and thoughts and then letting that person know you hear her or him.[8]

It is not unusual for us as parents and as people not to hear each other. There is a classic story of a parent and a child walking down a boardwalk and passing an ice cream stand. The parent wants an ice cream cone but cannot let himself or herself just have the cone. The parent decides the way to get a cone, guilt free, is to buy one for the child and one for the parent. When asked about the cone, the child says, "No, I don't want any ice cream. I want a hot dog." The parent says, "No, you don't want a hot dog. You want an ice cream cone." The parent cannot figure out why the child cries when given the cone instead of a hot dog. The child is not grateful in the parent's eyes.

Mutual recognition and relating do not happen in the example. Instead the parent treats the child like an object to satisfy the parent's narcissistic needs and projections. The parent wanted a cone and probably somewhere had a fantasy of wanting to walk down the boardwalk eating ice cream with his or her parent that never happened, so the parent makes it happen with the child. If the parent had been aware enough to recognize that he or she wanted the cone and could get a cone for the parent and a hot dog for the child, then mutual recognition and relating would have happened.

Because of gender polarity, mutual recognition rarely happens; gender polarity sets us up in a subject-object, one-up and one-down relationship where the dominant person does not have to listen to the other person because the dominant person is in power and knows best. A television show I watched as a child was *Father Knows Best*, and the father clearly was the head of the household and knew best for all in the family. The television show portrayed the values of its time.

What this means for May is that her internal snapshots devalued her abilities as a person and as a female. She had enough inner strength to break out of her parents' gender role model where her mother was a dependent housewife and her father was an independent worker. Unfortunately, this dependent-independent split lives inside her psyche. May did not have a model of how to feel equal with males and how to feel of value to herself as a female.

Thus, she was uncertain about how to relate to and compete with male coworkers without feeling guilty or inferior. If she competed with the men, then she felt guilty for being aggressive and stepping out of the bounds of her submissive female role model. If she stayed within her female role model, then she deferred to the men and felt inferior.

If a conflict arose, she would back down instead of dealing with it. If there was a problem at work, she would blame herself instead of searching for a solution. If someone got angry with her, she usually ended up in tears. Heaven forbid if she got angry at another person, particularly a male. If a man said he was right, then she decided immediately that she was wrong. She could not escape the sense that she was inferior because she was acting inferior. Anytime she began to get in touch with her inner strength she felt guilty and afraid she might come across as a "bitch." May struggled with how to understand and shed her cultural and religious conditioning.

Because May grew up in such a patriarchal family, church, and culture, she did not learn how to access her own strength and equality as a female. She had never had her value as a female recognized and validated. We as human beings need recognition and validation of our personhood and gender to feel good enough about ourselves. We receive this recognition and validation through the mirroring we receive from our parents, church, and culture.

Like a mirror, they reflect to children acceptance, value, morals, disapproval, and self-worth. Children take these mirrorings inside the self and create an image of the self. Mirroring is a major way we know who we are and receive ongoing validation of who we are. Pastoral theologian Carroll Saussy writes, "Through mirroring an ideology is formed, a worldview that informs the child as to what is expected of it and gives the child a sense of her or his place in mother's and father's lives and in the world."[9] I knew that my mirroring of May's abilities and self-worth had taken hold the day she asked me, "Is it all right not to be a martyr like my mother? Is it all right to focus on me?"

Our parents, church, and culture need to say it is good to be a strong female. Without this recognition and validation, May was cut off from her feminine soul. Her inner reality was dictated by cultural and religious norms that kept her from fully accessing her sense of self as a worthy, acceptable, capable, and equal person.

Writer Sue Monk Kidd describes her struggle to accept herself as an equal in God's eyes: "Steeped in a faith tradition that men had named, shaped, and directed, I had no alliance with what might be called the Sacred Feminine." Like May, she could not imagine that females are equal to males because she could not imagine that God could be female, too: "I tried briefly to imagine a God like me. God as female. But it was such a foreign notion."[10] Thus began Sue Monk Kidd's journey to discover the Sacred Feminine inside herself and to re-imagine God for herself. Her journey is powerfully described in her book *The Dance of the Dissident Daughter*.

There is a psychological explanation for why females find it difficult to imagine God as female and difficult to validate the female self. Sociologist and psychotherapist Nancy Chodorow, in her landmark book *Reproduction of Mothering*, described a process that has laid the groundwork for much further understanding about female psychology. In Western civilization the primary parent has predominantly been the mother; certain psychological dynamics are set up for males and for females that will not change until our way of parenting changes.

Of course, the traditional way of parenting with the mother as the primary parent supports gender polarity. Often the mother for biological reasons has been the primary parent. It was only in the mid-twentieth century that it was the mother who stayed at home and did not work. Also, it was only in the twentieth century that children were raised in a nuclear family (two parents and children) and not with extended family, a village, a tribe, or a town that helped to raise the children and that offered other adults with whom to identify. Our current way of parenting places most of the burden of rearing children on an isolated mother. In the early twenty-first century we find both traditional and new models of child rearing and being families. However, the focus is still on the mother as the primary parent.

Psychologically, this means that children bond primarily with the mother. Both male and female children learn their sense of identity from the mother, who is female. For females this sets up an intense bond, whether positive or negative, with the mother because the mother is the same sex as the female child. For female children, separating from the mother becomes difficult.

It is one reason females are more relational than males because females have more difficulty separating themselves from others' needs and wants. Like our mothers, we are programmed to take care of others, which requires the ability to relate. If a mother has internalized the cultural value that females are less than males, then the mother will mirror this sense of inferiority to her daughter.

To separate somewhat from the all-powerful mother, girls will turn to fathers for strength and identity different from the mother. A father's openness to having his daughter identify with him can be helpful for a girl. Psychiatrist Frank Pittman, author of *Man Enough*, writes,

If a man is going to raise a daughter to be a strong, secure woman, he must both like and respect women. His daughter's self-esteem depends upon his attitude. If the father believes that women are limited in what they can do in life, that women are weak and need to be protected by men, that "girls' stuff" is foolish, then his daughter is likely to grow up feeling limited, weak, and foolish. To a large degree, her successes in life and in love are in his hands. As he raises his daughter a father may have to question everything he thought he knew about gender, about the differences between men and women.[11]

However, often the father is not open because he has not learned how to relate with females and does not know what to do with his female child. Even if a father does know what to do, the cultural environment of gender polarity interferes with separation for females and for males. For females to separate and gain autonomy, they must defy their own femaleness.

If the female child is not able to get help from the father, she will be thrown back to the all-powerful bond with the mother or to a lifelong search for a male to validate her. Often I believe females turn to church not only for its moral and communal aspects but also for the worship of God the Father as a way to feel validated. The problem is that because there are not equal female God images, worshiping a male God continues to perpetuate the idea that females are not equal to males.

If there were equal male and female God images and if in our culture mother and father were equal, this would not be a problem. The child bases a part of identity on the gender likenesses with God. If female God images are less than male God images, then females are going to feel inferior to males. Sue Monk Kidd passionately states in reference to what a girl learns in church, "And most of all, as long as God 'himself' is exclusively male, she will experience the otherness, the lessness, of herself; all the pious talk in the world about females being equal to males will fail to compute in the deeper places inside of her."[12]

For male children to separate and find identity as males, they must break away from mother and join the world of father.

The problem is that under gender polarity, maleness is defined in opposition to femaleness, so the mother goes from being a person from whom the boy gets love to the person who can take away his maleness. Females become feared and must be kept in their place. Because the world of males is considered more powerful than the mother's world, boys grow up with a sense of power and privilege. Unfortunately, that sense of power and privilege is based on knowing that females are weak and inferior to males; it is not necessarily based on positive self-esteem. To be a man means not being a woman.

When the power of the mother is lessened by co-parenting and equality between the sexes, male and female children are able to learn how to get and give love from their parents rather than fear the mother and need to escape to the father. Psychiatrist Frank Pittman writes, "The biological distinction between a mother and a father ends completely at the point of weaning. After that, there is nothing a woman can do for a child that a father can't. And even before that, fathers can do a lot more than they usually do. The more involved the father is, the better he will bond to both his wife and his child."[13]

Both sexes need mutual images of God as Father and Mother to facilitate the process of self-discovery and self-assertion. Self-discovery entails taking the time and space to find out who one is and what one's feelings are apart from what others have said. It means discovering one's gifts and abilities even if those gifts do not fit defined gender roles. In our traditional gender roles males are not nurturing. The truth is that many males are sensitive and nurturing.

Self-discovery is the process of exploring, discovering, claiming, and validating this is who I am. Self-assertion is the process of taking who I am and, through initiative, expressing and making a space for the self in the world. It is feeling enough of value and worth that I want to make my place in the world, even that I deserve to have a place in the world. It is not just dreaming of writing a book but writing the book and getting it published. Traditionally, males have been given the privilege of place in the world and have been taught to be assertive. Females have been taught to accept second-class citizenship in the world and not to be assertive. Saussy comments, "Women have learned to sacrifice their own wants and needs and possibilities to 'better serve those they love.' In the process women can so lose touch with their abilities that they no longer hear the inner voice that clamors for those capacities to be used and the capacities remain idle."[14]

Both males and females need self-discovery and self-assertion. Simply stated, God as Mother enables the process of self-discovery and God as Father enables the process of self-assertion with neither process being better than the other. I vividly remember the beginnings of my process of self-discovering that femaleness is good and godly. In 1979, I was sitting in Trenton, New Jersey, watching Ntozake Shange's play *for colored girls who have considered suicide/when the rainbow is enuf* when I heard these lines: "I found God in myself and I loved her fiercely."[15] I felt fully recognized by God for the first time.

Tears came streaming down my cheeks, but I was not sure why. I was in my last year of seminary, and I was not particularly a feminist. I was not in a process of re-imaging God that I knew of. All of my seminary training told me that Shange's words were blasphemy because the words placed God above inside me and talked of God as "her." Yet her words touched me deeply in a place in my soul that had been lonely and empty. I felt a hunger begin inside me that haunted me until I learned how to feel my inner female soul and self. Sue Monk Kidd writes, "When we truly grasp for the first time that the symbol of woman can be a vessel of the sacred, that it too can be an image of the Divine, our lives will begin to pivot."[16]

The only way to internally overcome the devaluing images of being female and to feel equal, worthy, powerful, intelligent, sacred, and beautiful as a female is to learn to validate ourselves through self-discovery as females and to assert our value and selves in the world. This is a long and difficult process because the cultural gender polarity we live in creates tremendous resistance to female validation and equality. It requires focusing on what it means to be female—mind, body, and spirit. As long as God remains male, females will never feel equal.

Sue Monk Kidd asserts, "Women need to attack culture's oppression of women, for there truly is a godlike socializing power that induces women to 'buy in' or collude, but we also need to confront our own part in accepting male dominance and take responsibility where appropriate."[17] If we females wait for men to change the world, the world might change but not in our favor. The rest of this book is about how we as women must take responsibility for working through our own demeaning and devaluing images inside ourselves and learn how to assert ourselves in the world as equal human beings created in God's image.

3

The God I Worship Does Not Want Me to Say "No"

Sue is a wife, a mother of three sons, and a professional in the medical field. In her early forties, she takes pride in her home and is involved in her local Protestant church. God and church are important to her. In her spare time, she makes extra money for the family through selling her handicrafts. She is close to her parents and loves her husband. However, she feels unfulfilled and tired and wants to kill herself.

When Sue came to therapy, she had little idea of what she wanted for herself and felt guilty if she allowed herself to desire anything for herself alone. Saying "no" to others and "yes" to herself was not in her frame of reference. Sue described herself as "a caregiver who is falling apart now." She felt guilty and "stupid" for taking up my time and for being suicidal. She should not have allowed herself to get so discouraged, especially since she usually "toughs things out."

As Sue talked to me about her life, it made sense that she felt overwhelmed and trapped. She was blaming herself for a death at work that was nobody's fault. Her husband was working two jobs and considering a career change that would move the family. One son was having difficulties in school, her father had just had a heart attack, the house was on the market, and she worked full-time and took care of the home and children.

She had internalized the patriarchal cultural-religious orbit of meaning that defined her as the "all-giving mother and woman" who puts herself last. The part of herself that often is called the superego (what she should do, morals) was guided by standards set by men in her life—husband, sons, father, and Father God. Psychoanalyst Doris Bernstein notes that the typical female superego content is a commandment against autonomy and assertion. The ideal mother and woman is all-giving.[1] In other words, it is wrong to say "no" to others and "yes" to oneself.

Sue represents the female who is following the acceptable, traditional path for females of self-sacrifice and self-denial. Powerful messages in Western religion and society encourage females to live lives of sacrifice. It is okay for a female to have a self, to express herself, only after others' needs are met and only if the self does not challenge patriarchy. It is a false system that suppresses the female's true self, desires, and initiative. God is Father, and the husband is the head of the household.

Somewhere along the way, like Sue, many females wake up to realize that they feel trapped inside and that their cultural and religious images limit their ability to grow. As a good Christian woman who is supposed to obey her husband and honor God the Father, Sue did not know what to do when she felt suicidal. Feeling suicidal was not normal, and prayer was not relieving her fears or thoughts of death.

Why is Sue unable to say "no" to others and "yes" to herself? Traditionally, the female's identity and power come from self-sacrifice. Be the good girl, dutiful daughter, submissive wife, all-giving mother, and church handmaid. Females know how to sacrifice. Psychiatrist Natalie Shainess wrote a book called *Sweet Suffering* in which she attempts to address the masochism of females in our Western culture. Females have tended to deal with gender polarity through masochism, or self-sacrifice. Shainess writes, "And women, traditionally, have responded to their subjection by accepting it and attempting to fit into the expected passive mold in order to avoid trouble. They have turned their anger inward and adopted a 'suffering style'—the essence of masochism."[2]

Characteristics of masochism are overusing apology, accepting the word of others without thinking, being acquiescent and accommodating, rejecting praise, submitting to any authority, devaluing one's own thoughts and feelings, feeling threatened by others who have strong opinions, letting others off the hook, saying too much, not listening to and trusting one's own feelings and thoughts, having poorly maintained self-boundaries, experiencing supersensitivity to others' feelings and nonverbal expressions, mistaking dependence for love, and fearing abandonment to the point of doing anything to appease the other person. All of these characteristics closely match what it means to be a good Christian woman and wife.

In masochism created in reaction to gender polarity, the female is unable to express her own desire and agency. Her power comes from being powerless. Because the woman on some level senses that there is no escape from being subordinate, she has learned a way of coping that prevents harm. The masochist's aim is to appease and second-guess those she perceives have power over her so as to ward off the harm she fears and expects.[3] We have learned masochism from our mothers, who learned it from their mothers, who learned it from their mothers all the way back to five thousand years ago when patriarchy came into power.

Society was not always patriarchal. Before the rise of patriarchy, most cultures were matriarchal or worshiped both gods and goddesses. Women could rise to power, and there was a sharing of power between men and women. Anthropologists who study societies today have observed that societies with gender equality do not have gender polarity. Theologian Rosemary Radford Ruether writes:

> Societies with gender parity virtually always have creation myths that attribute the creation either to a female or a male and female together. By contrast male-dominant societies typically have male-only creation stories. Male-dominant societies also have rigid gender segregation and little parenting of smaller children. More egalitarian societies have less gender segregation. Gender lines are more fluid, and women and men do a

lot of work together. There is not a rigid concept of some work as only for men and only for women. Typically males are more integrated into early childcare in such societies as well.[4]

The belief is that the rise of patriarchy coincides with the realization of how procreation occurs. Five thousand years ago society shifted from hunter-gatherer to agrarian farmers who stayed in one place. People began to put two and two together about sex and procreation. Fathers realized that other men could father children with their wives. Fathers wanted control over who their children were, to be sure this is "my" child. Children and women became possessions rather than free people.

Warfare was invented to take what one could not produce. If people stayed put, then they could be attacked. Matriarchy and the goddess gave way to patriarchy and gender polarity through force and violence. A theory is that once men figured out the female power of procreation, they began to fear the female's creative power. Males counter this fear by becoming gods, who pass divinity from father to son. Females are below males because they need controlling. Females can tempt males sexually.

Through warfare, men prove worthiness by their willingness to sacrifice sons. Sons prove their worth by being willing to be sacrificed. Men prove worth through dying in warfare and women in dying for their men. Early revolutionary Christianity attempted to counter this prevalent Roman belief until Rome institutionalized Christianity. Rome's institutionalization of Christianity spread Christianity throughout the world, but early Christianity lost its early push for equality.

This patriarchal model remains in place today. Since the Industrial Revolution, the model has been changing. During the past two hundred years, each generation of fathers has had less authority than the last. The father left the home, farm, or small town business to go to work in the factory. Today this has expanded to the corporate level; men travel all over the country and world for their companies. Men had to leave the home because women had to stay to breast-feed the children. The arrival of better birth control and baby formula and bottles, a mid-twentieth-century phenomenon, has freed females to join the workforce outside the home.

The idea of masculinity shifted from the ability to father to the ability to make money and to provide for the family. Consequently, the man lost his connection to family, spouse, and children, and the mother became the primary parent. Until the Industrial Revolution, fathers imparted knowledge to children, gave them property, helped discipline children, taught morals, and provided an example through love, play, and care to children.

The loss of the father as a caregiver in the family has left child rearing up to females, which has created a problem for both mothers and fathers. With the father out of the house he is out of sight and out of mind. He has lost his child-rearing rights and has little influence on the children. The one role left for the father might be that of disciplinarian, but that continues to perpetuate gender polarity. For the mother, anything that goes wrong with the children is her fault. This situation creates problem for boys and girls as well.

Masculinity is passed on from father to son, not from mother to son. Without an active father, psychiatrist Frank Pittman believes a boy will not become a mature man. Pittman believes that where there is no father, a consistent father figure will help. Because women are the primary caregivers, mothers are given the power to give a male his masculinity or to take it away. A masculine mystique is created where females are either terrifyingly important or terrifyingly dangerous. If a woman becomes angry at a man, he fears that she is stripping him of his masculinity. It becomes difficult for males to tolerate female anger.

To protect themselves from the perceived all-powerful mother/woman, males around the age of ten begin to "break away" from mothers to join the superior male world rather than separate naturally. Separation implies toleration of difference, and separateness is the ability and desire to connect and disconnect at will. There is the awareness that he can get love from mother and be a man. "Breaking away" leads to the need to devalue, control, put down, be superior to mother and to females. Getting love from mother is wimpish, which means behaving like a female.

Without the presence of fathers, daughters and mothers become too merged into each other because they are the same sex. A girl "breaks away" from her mother by either withdrawing her real self and being "a good girl" or rebelling and becoming "a bad girl." Because of the fusion beween mother and daughter, if a mother devalues herself, her daughter will feel the same devaluing inside that her mother feels. In addition, often daughters experience their mothers valuing their brothers more because inside the mother is the cultural message that males are superior and females are inferior.

Girls need fathers to help them not devalue their mothers and themselves. Unfortunately, in our culture because males separate by devaluing females, it is difficult—if not impossible—for many fathers to treat females/daughters and spouses as equals. The tendency is to become overprotective when the daughter needs acceptance of her womanhood and self and acceptance of the desire to assert herself in the world.

I can remember that around age twelve, there was a change in how I was treated. I was no longer allowed to roam around the neighborhood as far as I used to go, and as I became a teenager, my curfew was earlier than that of my brothers. Although I knew the differences had to do with wanting to protect me from bad people in the world, I could feel my parents' anxiety eroding my sense of confidence that I could take care of myself. Both my parents and I fell prey to masochism.

A psychological process explains how masochism is passed on from mother to daughter. As I have mentioned earlier, the primary parent mirrors to the infant approval/disapproval, security/insecurity, love/hate, value/devalue, and so on. The infant learns to respond and react to the parent by what is mirrored. If the child is hungry and cries and the parent hears the hungry cries and feeds the baby, then the baby learns to trust that the self is recognized. If the child's hungry cries are ignored and possibly the child is spanked for crying, then the child learns that her or his needs are not recognized and learns not to trust.

The child will then attempt to learn the behavior that will get him or her fed. No parent is perfect. The object is to be a good enough parent who most of the time recognizes and attends to the infant's needs. In other words, the parent is able most of the time to differentiate between the cries of hunger, the cry of a wet diaper, and the cry of needing to be held and given attention.

Important to the development of a healthy self is the process of separation-individuation. In this process an infant is able to tolerate being separate from the parent, and the parent allows the infant space to be separate yet safe. We see the beginnings of this process in the game of peekaboo. Around age eighteen months to two years, a child will begin to explore the world. The child will wander a short distance from the parent and then will run back. The child also begins to say "no" to everything.

By virtue of experiencing separateness, as human beings we are then able to identify our own feelings, needs, wants, desires, abilities, and gifts and to act on them. This is the process of individuation. If an independent self is required for separation and our culture does not enable females to have separate selves, then mothers will have difficulty allowing their children to separate, and the children will have to "break away." During adolescence, this separation-individuation process is revisited.

Because of the close bond between mother and daughter, this process of separation-individuation is even more difficult. A negative cycle of recognition is developed where the female infant responds to the mother's needs rather than to her own needs. Often the mother will place her needs on the female infant. This is the origin of the female child living out the mother's unfulfilled fantasies and life. Usually, the mother's feelings are negative, embodying the sociocultural message that females are inferior and dependent on males for their self-esteem and survival.

In a negative cycle of recognition the person either has to be who the mother wants her to be or reacts against the mother. Neither position leads to separation-individuation. To react against the mother, the child must repress the positive feelings toward the mother, which cuts the child off from love and care. If the child submits to the mother, then the child receives the mother's love and care at the expense of the child's wants and needs. Only mirroring that recognizes the infant's needs, wants, and unique self leads to separation-individuation.

Both positions—reacting and/or deferring to the mother—lead to self-denial. Self-denial manifests itself predominantly through unhealthy dependence. The child is so afraid of losing the mother's approval and presence, positive or negative, that the child remains bound to the mother and never separates. Unhealthy dependence leads to self-sacrificing giving and help-lessness. To work through unhealthy dependence, females have to struggle with their relationship with their mothers.

It is a complicated struggle for females who are raised by the traditional, passive dependent female and distant father. If the mother's source of power is in self-sacrifice, then discovering and asserting self will make the daughter different from the mother. There is the fear of destroying the bond with the internalized mother, who provides identity to the daughter.

As Shainess indicates, females' self-denial and unhealthy dependence often lead to masochism. Masochism is the active seeking for or facilitation of psychic pain and suffering that lead to self-abnegation and subordination. Pain is not sought for pleasure; it is sought because suffering defines the self and keeps the daughter connected to the mother. Luise Eichenbaum and Susie Orbach write, "The girl learns her social role from her mother, as her mother did from her own mother."[5] Success and good feelings are to be avoided at all costs because they threaten the bond of self-sacrifice. This is one of the reasons that hus-bands have such a difficult time getting their wives to leave the children to go out for a good time.

Through self-sacrifice, the child can feel powerful over the internal maternal snapshot that is controlling her life. "One can always omnipotently guarantee rejection—love is much chancier. If one can securely enjoy disappointment, it is no longer possible to be disappointed."[6] The special sense of suffering compensates for the self-denial. Obedience takes the place of assertion and aggression. Instead the aggression is directed at the self. Daughters internalize this way of relating because this is the way that females for centuries have dealt with the domination-submission cultural structure of gender polarity. Females trick themselves into believing they are morally superior to males rather than recognizing the reality of their oppression.

The church participates in these bonds of love when it encourages a theology of self-sacrifice and limits images of God to patriarchal symbols. The church's emphasis on the sanctity and virtue of mothers makes it difficult to even consider re-imaging the female role in church and society. Self-sacrifice is equated with being Christlike.

Pride, the opposite of self-sacrifice, is understood theologically to be the primary sin of humanity. We forget that Jesus died on the cross to save us from sin so that we do not have to die on the cross. For a male who focuses almost completely on himself, pride is a sin. For a female who does not even focus on herself, pride is salvation rather than sin. Jesus called us to love our neighbors as ourselves. Thus, each person is to have a self. For most females to have a self, we need to learn to have positive pride in ourselves.

Too often guilt sets in for females the minute we focus on self and our own needs and wants. Real guilt has to do with feeling remorse when we violate a moral law—when we do a wrong. Unhealthy guilt occurs when we violate an ideal picture of ourselves. For example, I should meet everyone's needs; I should never hurt or disappoint another person; I should give completely of myself because that is what Jesus did; I should always please. Realistically, these are impossible demands.

Sue became suicidal because she violated her internal ideal picture, which emphasized that she was never to hurt another person but was always to assume the blame. Rationally, she knew that patients die and sometimes unexpectedly. She had done no wrong, yet a death had occurred. The ideal pictures inside most females do not know how to understand the things in life that are beyond control. Sue got caught in a never-ending cycle of guilt that constantly blamed herself. Every time she attempted to think her way out of this negative cycle she encountered her internal conflict.

The religious-cultural snapshots inside Sue reminded her that she must give all of herself to fix wrongs. She must take the blame if the family of the patient felt a need to lay blame as a way to handle grief over the loss of the loved one. Yet the thinking part of herself recognized that death happens and only God knows when it is someone's time to die.

Understanding the dynamics of self-sacrifice helped me in my work with Sue. I knew that I needed to provide Sue the space to discover her own self and feelings. I needed to mirror to her my recognition of who she was so that she could feel herself validated and could claim herself. To help her deal with her guilt over focusing on herself, I gave her some knowledge and insight about why females have difficulty saying "no." I listened to her theological concerns about her role as a good follower of Jesus and offered her alternate interpretations. I reminded her that even Jesus needed time and space for himself to rest and pray.

I listened to Sue and offered her a space where she could sort through her devaluing snapshots, attend to her feelings, and stop a moment to consider what she wanted for herself. I gently questioned the "male" standards of her superego wondering if there were more options. Whenever she started to focus too much on another person's needs, I focused her back on herself. I encouraged her to imagine how she would like to be and to live.

Because God was very important to her, I encouraged her to imagine how God would respond to her and how God would want her to be. Would God really be mad at her for being suicidal, as she feared, or would God be compassionate toward her pain? Her guilt at feeling suicidal added to her depression and kept her from exploring her suicidal feelings. Did God want her to sacrifice herself to the point of suicide, or did God want her to love herself? Was God only a God of judgment? Could not God be a God of grace and judgment? What would grace be for Sue? Would not God care about her as much as God cared about her husband and sons?

Six months into therapy, Sue came into the counseling session acting very excited. She said, "I've begun to grow wings on my back!" An important image for Sue was the image of God's angels. She had discovered that she had her own angel wings. With these wings she could begin to fly free wherever she wanted. With these angel wings, Sue recognized that God valued her, too, as a female. For Sue, angels were female.

Sue asked for a female therapist because she was afraid that a male therapist would tell her that she was responsible for the world, just as the male pastors of her church usually told her. Instinctively, Sue knew she needed to have her female self recognized, supported, explored, and validated. Given the gender polarity in her superego that idealized males and devalued females, she needed to experience a female who valued herself and would help her value herself. Being with another female who understood the importance of mutual recognition lessened the fear inside Sue so that she could begin a conversation with her rigid superego and work through her negative snapshots and add positive snapshots, such as her female angel image.

She came to realize that the death at work was not her fault. Feeling concern for the patient did not mean having to be responsible for the patient's life. People die. At home, she realized she needed help, so she asked for help from her husband and her sons. Sue recognized that much stress was coming from the reality that she did not want to move. Even if it meant her husband had to modify his career dream, she was not going to move. They could get over the death of a dream, but her death, by suicide, would be permanent. She took seriously her needs and her limits. Sue realized she was worthy of living. She did not have to be a martyr. It was okay to say "no."

For Sue's depression to lift, she had to learn it was acceptable to desire things for herself, to express her needs and wants to her family, and to find a new image of God that both upheld her more traditional values and upheld the freedom to choose for herself. Sue had to rework her idealized image of maleness and her devalued image of femaleness, a form of gender polarity. God is Father for her; yet through the femaleness of the angel, Sue was able to equalize more than before her relationship with males. Angels with wings are free to go wherever they want.

The therapeutic space that gave privilege to Sue's female voice that was crying, "I can't go on like this anymore," offered her a place to grow to appreciate a broader view of herself. Being female could mean playing as well as working. It gave her a place to imagine God in a new way. She could have wings, dreams, and decisions, as her husband did. Expressing her voice and choices did not mean usurping his position of power but offered both of them the opportunity to be partners and helpmates for each other. Sue was able to become open to God's redemptive possibilities present for her and to move from a position of believing her soul to be bad and condemned to one of recognizing the good and bad inside herself and trusting in the newness that God offered her.

4

The God I Worship Depresses Me and Denies Me Anger

"I don't know if I'm angry. I can't get angry at him. I don't want to hurt him. It's okay for me to hurt. I'd rather that I hurt than risk losing him. It's not Christian to get angry." Gail's words echo the words of many females who do not know how to express anger in a healthy way.

The cultural and religious taboos against anger are so great in Western civilization that many females do not know when they are angry. Parents teach daughters to be passive, dependent, pleasing, and loving, especially in relation to men. Harriet Lerner, the author of *The Dance of Anger*, writes, "The direct expression of anger, especially at men, makes us unladylike, unfeminine, unmaternal, sexually unattractive, or more recently, 'strident.'"[1]

The proscription against female anger can be understood within the broader context of women's subordinate role in society.[2] As nurturers and caregivers, women do not like to threaten relational ties. The fear is that anger will cause a break in the relationship. For many years, there was the realistic fear that if a woman became angry, she could lose her economic support. A female friend recently told me that if she were economically independent of her husband, she would feel freer to be angry with him. Females learn to fear expression of anger because it usually causes disapproval.

As a young girl, I had no difficulty expressing my anger. I was forthright with my anger and used it as a way to fend off my brothers and protect myself. I got angry when I felt something was not right. It was my way of saying, "You are not going to mistreat me," or "I need for you to listen to me." Somewhere along the way of growing up, I buried my anger, except in rare instances when it would pop out. Then I felt ashamed or guilty. As I neared adolescence and then beyond, anytime I became angry my brothers called me Mean Mary.

For years being called Mean Mary kept me quiet. I did not want to be perceived as mean. Being mean was bad. It was not until I was in my thirties and doing my own personal therapy and reading about female psychology that I began to realize that I had silenced my anger.

Healthy anger enables us to declare our separateness, differences, and need to make changes. Anger is a vehicle for change when it is used in a responsible way for self-growth. When we are angry, we assume a position of strength that makes a statement about the self. Anger can be denied, repressed, or expressed in ineffectual ways. There are ways of expressing or not expressing anger that keep a person stuck in behavior patterns that prevent change and often lead to negative self-thoughts.

When I expressed anger as an adult, it usually came out as an explosion. Explosive anger is unhealthy for all. I usually shocked and hurt the person(s) I was angry with and then felt bad inside myself. Not knowing how to express my anger in a healthy manner supported my feelings of low self-worth.

Anger is not encouraged in females in our society. Consequently, many women have difficulty expressing anger. At the same time, anger is necessary for the separation-individuation process. Anger is a signal that something needs changing. Anger is emotional energy, and healthy aggression is the expression of that energy. Anger and aggression can be positive and negative. They are positive when they release energy leading persons to make constructive changes to the self. They are negative when they overload emotions that get trapped into cyclic processes of resentment, blaming, rage, hostility, passive-aggressiveness, self-hatred, and violence.

In a nutshell, anger is an emotional response consisting of a physiological state of bodily arousal, a cognitive state defining the arousal, and an energizing state with drive and power. Physically feeling, thinking about, and experiencing the power and capacity of anger to lead to change and growth can be frightening to females who are not used to such intense feelings. Our bodies have two subsystems: the parasympathetic system calms the body, and the sympathetic system prepares the body to deal with intense experiences such as anger and fear. We can operate out of only one system at a time. This is why after feeling angry or scared, we will need a while to calm down. We have to pause first before we can shift systems and begin the process of calming down.

This knowledge of the two subsystems is important. Many females expect that they should be able to get over anger right away. When I first began to let myself feel anger again, I had to tell myself that the powerful feelings are normal and healthy. When we are sad, we feel tender and teary. When we are angry, we feel a powerful rush of emotion inside. Healthy anger tells us something is not all right and aims to make a change. Unhealthy anger aims to injure. I had to remind myself that the feelings are not bad, but I should endeavor to express my feelings in helpful ways, not harmful ways. If I wanted to calm down, then I had to work at letting my body take its time to calm down.

If anger is not ventilated or resolved, it does not dissolve. Instead it is denied, displaced, converted, or destructively emerges. More self-differentiated people are more capable of experiencing and expressing anger. David Augsburger commented, "Constructive anger energizes the person, interrupts the denial process, expresses needs, defends against imposition, mobilizes coping behaviors and assists the person in discriminating the character of relationship requiring renegotiation."[3]

Why are females reluctant to accept the reality that anger is a part of any human being's life? The roots for women's prohibition against anger lie in early psychological development and are reinforced by church and society. As part of the feminine socialization process, anger is discouraged in infants, and girls learn to repress and suppress their anger and aggression. Most infants are raised by mothers. Since most women carry the unconscious internal snapshot that anger and aggression are wrong, unfeminine, and possibly sinful, mothers pass this snapshot on to their daughters who are the "same" as they are.

The mother identifies her femaleness in her daughter and projects onto her daughter her own feelings. If the mother cannot cope with her own feelings of anger and aggression or her own needs and wants, the mother will reject these feelings and needs from her infant daughter. A negative cycle of mutual recognition is developed, and the infant learns to recognize what the mother is comfortable with rather than what the infant feels and needs.

It is natural for the infant to be aggressive in exploring her environment. For healthy growth she needs acceptance of both nurture and aggression. If her mother is afraid of anger and aggression because she has repressed the feelings inside herself, then the mother will deny these feelings and needs in her daughter. Girls are thought of as sweet whereas boys are regarded as sour. The daughter will learn to fear her anger and needs and will hide these parts of herself away so that she can maintain her connection with her mother. Most females have a photo album that we present to society and a hidden or buried photo album of which we may or may not be aware but which, in its dormant state, inhibits our growth and self-expression. The female infant's separation-individuation process becomes modified because anger and aggression are necessary for self-discovery and self-assertion.

Additionally, whenever the primary caregiver is gone from the infant for any length of time, the infant experiences anxiety over the separation. The infant is totally dependent on the care of the parent. The infant wants to know where her provider and protector is. If the separation goes on for a while, the infant's anxiety will turn naturally to anger. The infant is asking, "Where are you?" If the parent returns soon enough and is able to tolerate the infant's protests, then the infant learns that separation is a normal part of life and that loved ones return. Trust is developed.

If the parent is uncomfortable with the infant's anger, then the infant has a difficult time learning that anger is one of the ways we tolerate temporary separations from loved ones. If anger is denied and avoided, it keeps the illusion alive that everything will work out fine by keeping the connection intact with the loved one. The problem is that often in life everything is not fine, and anger is God's gift to us to enable us to tolerate temporary separations and make necessary changes to better our lives and relationships. Anger is necessary to the development of trust, and we need trust to have faith in self, others, and God.

Because of this hidden photo album that tells us to deny anger, most females feel hurt instead of expressing anger or protest. Lerner asserts, "Hurt, in contrast to anger, emphasizes the relational 'we' rather than the autonomous 'I.'"[4] Because anger involves the feeling of being separate, alone, and different, and because females are afraid of losing connections, the feeling of anger will stir up separation anxiety and an unconscious fear of loss of the relationship. These fearful feelings cause the female to attempt to reestablish the relationship with the person with whom she is angry by several behaviors other than anger.

She might cry, criticize herself, express hurt, act withdrawn and depressed, act as if nothing is wrong while sulking, or apologize if she did express outward anger. This dynamic is part of the reason it is so difficult for females to believe a relationship is abusive and then to leave the abusive relationship.

Females are socialized to be relational so that relationships are more important than having a self. This leads to de-selfing. De-selfing occurs when the female gives up too much of herself, her thoughts, wants, beliefs, desires, and ambitions, in order to maintain a relationship.[5] Although expressing anger and having a self would lead to a more intimate and stronger relational bond, females find it extremely difficult to overcome their conditioning against not expressing anger.

A part of the role of the female in relation to the male is to be the weaker sex who is ladylike and who protects the male from her anger so that he might feel stronger. Unfortunately, acting as the weaker sex and participating in de-selfing create repressed anger that leaves the female vulnerable to depression, masochism, addictions, abuse, and other emotional problems.

Females are raised to believe that there are two options for us in regard to anger and aggression. A female is either a "nice lady," who stays silent, tearful, self-critical, and apologetic, or a "bitch," who nags, blames, or gets into an ineffectual cycle of anger. My brothers who called me Mean Mary were experiencing me as the "bitch" who needed to be put in her place. The "nice lady" category protects the other person from anger and attempts to preserve harmony. The "bitch" category elicits disapproval and keeps one stuck in the same behavior pattern. Anger is vented but not resolved.

Both categories blur the female clarity of self and ensure that change for self-growth and change in the relationship do not take place.[6] For self-growth to take place, females have to become self-responsible for learning to express anger and other feelings in healthy ways. Females have to learn to work at tolerating the separateness that comes with expressing anger. However, self-discovery and self-assertion by females often are felt as acts of betrayal against self, relationships, and generations of family women.

The real issue for females in expressing anger and assertion is independence. Lerner makes the point: "Independence means that we clearly define our own selves on emotionally important issues, but it does not mean emotional distance."[7] Anger emerges as an act of self-proclamation. Because of the rules of family and society as well as the female psychological makeup, the female struggles to define herself apart from the wishes and expectations of others. Not expressing anger leads to emotional distance because the female represses and denies her true self in not sharing her true feelings. This sets up a false relationship that functions through the female and male playing roles rather than relating. Perhaps I can illustrate these dynamics through my work with Gail and offer suggestions through her story about how to learn to overcome the fear of expressing anger.

Gail, a "nice Christian woman," is a prime example of someone caught in the bind between nurturing relationships and expressing anger that females experience. She is a thirty-three-year-old white female who is a successful middle management businesswoman. She is very active in her church and has contemplated going into the ministry. Gail is the oldest of three, having two younger brothers. Her mother is a traditional homemaker. Throughout her childhood, she shadowed her mother with "Mom and me doing this and that together." Gail's mother shunned anger in females but put up with the rage of her husband and sons and at times their destruction of objects. Gail describes her father as a workaholic who considers her special, yet is emotionally distant from her.

She initially came to therapy because she was having difficulty sustaining relationships with men. She had yet to have a relationship with a man that lasted several months before either he or she ended it. During the course of ten months of therapy, we have talked about Gail's need to be in control, her need to please others, particularly males, and her inability to express anger.

My therapeutic process with her is focused on mirroring— encouraging her to notice and say what she feels, to look at cultural and family messages, to explore her family history of anger and rage, to let go of controlling and pleasing behaviors, and to test alternate ways of relating. The extent of Gail's fear of anger became obvious to me when she related to me her latest relationship experience. She was having a long-distance relationship with Bill and felt positive about how things were going. He came into town and wined and dined her. After a wonderful night on the town and dinner, Bill told her while they were having dessert that he had decided the relationship was over. Gail was shocked and reacted little to his pronouncement.

When I asked her what she was feeling, she said, "I can't get angry at him. I don't want to hurt him. If I don't get angry, maybe he'll come back, but he hasn't called." We talked about her not expressing anger as a way to protect herself from her pain and disappointment. It was a way to hold on to the fantasy that the relationship still existed. She said several telling things, for example, "I'm tired of building character. I want to build strength and beauty." One way in the past that Gail compensated for her hurt and disappointment was to see them as building character. Character building is becoming wearisome. What she needs is the building of strength, self-worth, and self-affirmation as a female. Expressing her anger in a healthy way will lead Gail to experience self-worth and self-affirmation.

As we talked, Gail said, "I felt anger, but I couldn't express it. I couldn't throw something at him." The one time Gail got angry at home, she threw a glass of water at her brother and stormed out of the dining room. The family did not understand her actions and did not approve of her angry display. She still feels guilty about her outburst. When I suggested she could be angry at Bill and not throw something at him, she launched into talking about what it was like to live in a house with an angry father and angry brothers who made her want to blend into the carpet. She began to relive a childhood scene of violence between her father and one of her brothers.

It was clear to me that Gail was afraid of expressing her anger because her only model of being angry was a violent and rageful one and she did not want to be angry that way. I shared with her that anger did not have to be violent. We talked of healthy ways she could be angry. Because anger stirs up intense feelings, she could fantasize throwing water at Bill. Part of the purpose of fantasy is for us to be able to let off steam without hurting anyone and get to a point where we can safely interact with others. She could yell and scream in her car or into a pillow. She could journal her feelings. She could have said, "Bill, what you said makes me angry, particularly because there was no warning. Why didn't you tell me this before wining and dining me?"

We decided that if she needed to, she could write him a letter expressing her anger. The purpose of writing Bill would be not to get him back but to share her anger and get it out of her system so that she could move forward. The English word "aggressive" comes from the Latin word *adgredi*, which means "to go to," "to approach." Writing a letter is a way for Gail to approach her feelings and provide an avenue for her to move forward with her anger and her life. She might write several drafts before finding a way to express her anger in a healthy way. Gail reached a point where she wrote and sent a letter to Bill expressing her anger. I let her know that I was proud of her.

It is apparent to me that Gail learned from her mother to shun anger, and her family did not encourage the expression of anger in females. Gail learned from her mother to deny her anger and aggression, and her mother learned from her family. Gail shared with me that she had talked with her mother about anger and found out that her mother had witnessed her father yelling at her brother. The incident had so frightened her that she had not spoken of the incident or her feelings to anyone until speaking to Gail.

Females are born capable of expressing anger and aggression. An infant wails angry cries when indicating hunger or the need for a diaper change or protesting separation from a loved one. Without anger and aggression we could not survive and thrive in this world. We are born with the two primary drives of love and aggression. We need to have the ability to engage others and to act on others to get our needs met. Unfortunately in Western civilization, these two drives have become split down gender lines and roles. Boys are to be aggressive and girls are to be loving. The church has supported this split.

Traditionally, the church views anger as sinful evidence of our fallen nature rather "than as vital energy for living productively when channeled appropriately." The patriarchal stance of the church has supported women's submissive, subordinate role as individuals in society and in families. Women are caught in the Greek mind-body split; females are associated with the inferior body where emotions reside. When we are connected to the Hebraic unity of mind, body, and spirit, we realize that anger is rooted in God's creation. "We are created with the capacity for power, anger and assertiveness. These are essential parts of the image of God in us. . . . Authentic, creative anger unites loving power and powerful love to demand justice in relationship and mutuality in the resolutions of differences."[8]

Females need a theology with images of God that address the conflict between society's view of women as nurturers and women's need to be more angry and assertive in order to have full selves. Females need a theology that offers a way for their intrapsychic split to be healed. Females need a theology with new symbols, names, and images of God that will have power and liberation for women. The traditional images do not resolve the tensions in many females' lives.

Theologian Beverly Harrison believes that historically, women have not been more passive than men. Women have been doers, creators, and risk takers. Harrison writes, "Women have been the doers of life-sustaining things, the 'copers,' those who understand that the reception of the gift of life is no inert thing, that to receive this gift is to be engaged in its tending, constantly."[9] Females have built community from the beginning of time as well as created tools and discovered better ways of surviving.

Harrison's work is on understanding anger as the radical activity of love and an imaginative act of hope. Anger can enable human beings to define self. Anger signals that all is not well in our relationships with self and other. To be in healthy relationships, we need a solid sense of self. Constructive anger provides the impetus to deepen relationships and bring forth community. When anger is seen as a deadly sin, it causes us to inhibit the power of love rather than to understand anger as a signal, a call from God, for change and transformation.[10] When everything is not right in our relationships and lives, the energy from anger can enable us to hope for a new way of being and to then act on this hope.

We have been taught to believe that anger is destructive. Unhealthy anger can be destructive, leading to violence. However, the issue is not whether anger is bad, but what we should do with our anger. Harrison writes, "The moral question is not 'what do I feel?' but rather 'what do I do with what I feel?'"[11] I will never forget my therapist telling me that feelings were neutral, neither good nor bad. It was what I chose to do with my feelings that mattered.

Harrison believes that we have come close to killing real love because we have understood anger to be a deadly sin. In real loving relationships people have to negotiate how to live with each other. When someone is gone and we need him or her, anger occurs. When we have unmet needs, we feel angry. When the relationship needs to change, anger is there to facilitate the change. Without anger, love can become stagnant. When anger is denied, we become apathetic rather than seekers of justice in the world.

This traditional belief about anger cuts us off from our ability to create self, to change, and to act in a just way. Anger can be a powerful way of caring that provides energy and focus for change and justice. When we are angry, we ask for the other to recognize our presence and value. It is a way of saying, "Hear me and speak with me." Without constructive anger that is motivated by love, relationships and community are stunted. Harrison powerfully states, "The important point is that where feeling is evaded, where anger is hidden or goes unattended, masking itself, there the power of love, the power to act, to deepen relation, atrophies and dies."[12]

Harrison bases her understanding of the radical activity of love on the life of Jesus. Jesus understood loving activity to be what leads to mutual relating and to justice. Jesus stood in solidarity with the outcasts of society and expressed anger if necessary to get his point across. In Mark 3:1–6, Jesus challenged the Pharisees who were waiting to catch him in the act of healing on the Sabbath. Healing on the Sabbath broke Jewish law. Jesus contended that it was more lawful to save a life even if it broke the law. Then the scripture recorded, "He looked around at them with anger; he was grieved at their hardness of heart and said to the man, 'Stretch out your hand.'" Jesus healed the man's hand, and the Pharisees went away plotting to kill Jesus. Jesus used his anger as a way to enable him to have the strength to heal the man's hand. Carroll Saussy and Barbara J. Clarke, in their article "The Healing Power of Anger," write, "Jesus chose anger that leads eventually to freedom, a freedom he won by using anger to bring about change."[13]

Despite the fact that there is room in the Bible for the expression of anger, females have to deal with the reality that religion, society, and family have prohibitions against expressing anger. To express anger, a woman has to develop enough of a self to withstand the anxiety associated with separating by taking a stand for herself. Jesus was able to use anger to bring about change because he stood up to the Pharisees. Harriet Lerner writes concerning females:

> The expression of legitimate anger and protest is more than a statement of dignity and self-respect. It is also a statement that one will risk standing alone, even in the face of disapproval or the potential loss of love from others. For our female patients, this requires a particular degree of courage. Not only have women been taught that their value, if not their very identity, rests largely on their loving and being loved, but also, even

more to the point, many women have not achieved the degree of autonomous functioning that would permit them to stand separate and alone in the experience of their anger.[14]

The tendency is to allow the anxiety to soften or repress the anger. Females who are working on discovering and expressing their anger need to be aware that they are works in progress. They will resist expressing anger, and they must take intentional steps to become more comfortable with anger.

This chapter on anger is key to the entire process of liberating God imges and re-imaging God. To use our imagination to re-image something, we have to step outside the norm. Re-imaging God images is going to undoubtedly stir up anger. Author of *A God Who Looks Like Me*, Patricia Reilly writes, "Women are afraid of the anger that may surface as their eyes are opened to the wider reality of a woman's life. They have been taught to be nice, not angry. At some deep level women know that to explore their religious past is to touch a deep rage within them—the accumulated rage of generations of women who were taught to resign themselves to the pain and suffering inherent in a woman's life."[15] Any group of people silenced and stymied against free expression of thoughts and feelings will have to go through a time of anger. It is part of a grieving process that lets go of the old way and prepares ground for a new way of being.

When I first started the process of exploring my religious and cultural heritage as a female, I got angry. For a long time I am not sure I was aware I was angry, but I was. When I did become aware of my anger, I felt guilty and sinful about feeling angry. Then I felt justified in my anger and was angry at everybody and everything. Particularly, I was angry at the church and at men.

Since females are socialized to depend on men to rescue and/or complete them, a woman who finally realizes that no man can do this is going to feel angry at men for a while. The anger helps the female to create a space in which to explore and come to know herself; then she can complete herself and be able to become a true partner.

The tendency at this point of anger is to bail out and go back to being compliant or to get stuck here and to remain angry at everyone forever. Either response avoids dealing with discovering and expressing who one is. Women are angry for different lengths of time, depending on how deeply wounded they are. It is not unusual to have flare-ups of intense anger from time to time. It is very likely that the males in your life and the females who have yet to begin self-exploration will attempt to entice you back to the way things were. It is difficult for any of us to tolerate anger, much less anger from a loved one. Hold firm to your resolve, but have some compassion for the friends and family members who may not understand.

To help yourself continue on your journey and to receive support in working on discovering and expressing anger, find safe places to recover and work through the anger, to continue discovering your own wants and needs. Having a female friend who is going through a similar process or who is ahead of you on this journey is a help. Finding someone to listen and understand is important. Becoming involved in individual or group therapy centered on issues of self-discovery and self-assertion can be invaluable. Seek a female therapist who is aware of the need for females to re-image not only self but also God images and who values females discovering their anger.

A women's support or spirituality group can be a safe place to uncover and liberate myths about anger and religion. Having a group of people to whom to be accountable offers a place where you can journey with others who can let you know when you have gone overboard in projecting your anger onto men and others. I participated in a women's spirituality group for three years where through conversation and creative expression we talked about ourselves and our spiritual needs as women. It was a wonderful experience, although at times a painful one. Some women find book groups helpful through reading and discussing Lerner's *The Dance of Anger*, Kidd's *The Dance of the Dissident Daughter*, Reilly's *A God Who Looks Like Me*, or any of a number of other books.

You may want to keep a journal about your anger. At one point in my life I created a list of daily questions to answer: What am I feeling? Am I mad, glad, sad, or afraid? If I am feeling angry, what is the source of my anger? What would help me to express my anger? What do I want to do today? What needs do I have that are not getting met, and how can I get these needs met? I journaled about anything that I felt it would be helpful to write about. I allowed myself to scream into a pillow or alone in the car or house or wherever I felt safe as a way to get the anger and rage out of my system.

At some point it became very important for me to find a way to talk about God through a theology that was life-giving and affirming to me as a female and that allowed me to explore and express my anger. If we do not spend time liberating our biblical and theological understandings of anger, then we remain caught in the old theology and traditions. The old theology and traditions will continue to eat away at any progress made toward re-imaging.

Most traditional theologies are based on a hierarchical understanding of relationship. Usually, we translate this hierarchy as God, male, female, child, in that order. Suppose, though, our relationship with God was as mutual partners. Throughout the Hebrew Scriptures, God renegotiated the covenant with the people of Israel. God created male and female to be helpmates for each other.

Jesus focused on loving and just relationships rather than hierarchy. He broke most hierarchical laws by teaching and speaking with females, by healing people with leprosy, by eating with people who were poor, by working on the Sabbath, and more. The emphasis in both the Hebrew and the Christian Scriptures is on loving and just relationships. To relate in a loving and just manner means to be more interested in valuing and understanding a person, in enabling a person to fulfill her or his God-given potential, than in adhering to hierarchy or rules.

Early on in my journey the theologian Sallie McFague proved helpful to me. She believes that we use various metaphors to converse about God. Traditionally, these metaphors have been patriarchal. Since there are a number of metaphors used to describe God, why not create several new metaphors that will help humanity's relationship with God during this particular historical time? She writes, "The assumption here is that all talk of God is indirect: no words or phrases refer directly to God, for God-language can refer only through the detour of a description that properly belongs elsewhere."[16]

In other words, God is mystery and is beyond description, although we use metaphors and images to attempt to talk about our experience and knowledge of God.

Her metaphorical theology is an attempt to offer new models of God that are not restrictive, that are inclusive of all of humanity and of nature, and that deal with the need for new models for humanity to be able to understand the interconnection between God and ourselves. McFague describes her new models of God in her book *Models of God*. Concretely, God is viewed as Mother, Lover, and, Friend. In humanity these images call for self-motivation and social motivation, empathy (concern, care, and nurture), and the self as an artist who weaves and spins out the construction of a society and a self from conflicting desires and complexes of thoughts and feelings.

Her model perceives God as Mother (Parent) of the world. In keeping with the understanding that no one metaphor describes God totally, McFague believes, "To speak of God as mother is to invite us to consider some qualities associated with mothering as one partial but perhaps illuminating way of speaking of certain aspects of God's relationship to us." The world is the body of God. As Mother of the world, God is on the side of life, healing and reuniting.[17] Mother God impartially wills existence and fulfillment for all beings. This is a personal and relational God who is involved in the lives and life of her creation. Since the world is seen as the body of God, it requires humanity's responsible cooperation to take appropriate care of God's body.

As Mother, God represents the "good enough mother" who encourages independence in her offspring. For women whose wounded selves began in infancy, a new understanding of mother as capable of allowing independence can be healing and freeing. As Mother, God is both creator and judge, who is capable of anger to provide for her children when fulfillment is blocked.[18] All have a right to existence and nourishment. Mother God gets angry at wrongs that interfere with her children's and world's achievement of fulfillment. There are no first-, second-, or third-class citizens in this model of God. This model of God allows females to express constructive anger and nurture, and it fully values female existence.

God as Lover exemplifies the model of love demonstrated in the story of Jesus. God as Lover finds value in all of creation. God, humanity, and the world have an intimate, loving relationship where "in the eyes of the beloved, one sees a different image of oneself: one sees a valuable person." God as Lover has to do with the passionate, deep feeling, "moving power of love in the universe" that is genuine love, which endures through barriers and difficulties because the beloved is valuable even when the value may not be seen.[19] What words of healing and good news for females who struggle with feeling internal and external value!

As Lover, God is the source of healing power, which undercuts the body-spirit split and binds together the wounds in our bodies. "In other words, God as lover and healer is at one with God as mother and judge in insisting on the health of bodies as the condition of other kinds of well-being."[20] God as Lover connects us to the physical, psychological process of healing.

God as Friend bases relationships on freedom. Friendship bonds two people together by free choice in a reciprocal relationship. The freedom to be in relationship is based on trust.[21] God as Friend speaks to the relationship of trust that is built between people engaged in a mutual process of trying to become fully who each one is with all of one's feelings and God-given gifts. Women are not bound solely to be nurturers.

In true friendship we must strive to end gender polarity, sexism, racism, and any type of relationship that places another person in a one-down position. Friendship is focused on relationships and interrelationships that cause the well-being of others and the world. We are called to be companions, friends, and advocates with God to support God's creation. McFague writes, "If God is the friend of the world, the one committed to it, who can be trusted never to betray it, who not only likes the world but has a vision for its well-being, then we as the special part of the body—the imago dei—are invited as friends of the Friend of the world to join in that vision and work for its fulfillment."[22]

McFague's model of God follows the trinitarian model of Father, Son, and Holy Spirit (in inclusive language, Creator, Redeemer, and Sustainer). Mother God demands the right of all to existence and nourishment. Lover God values all passionately and gets angry when injustice occurs. God as Friend requires that God and humanity are to be companions united with one another in fulfilling God's creation and well-being.

Why have I put this theological model at this place in the book? It is my opinion that female theologians, like other minority theologians, needed to feel angry before new theological models could be written. Their anger helps to take a stand against the traditional theologies. With the advent of the feminist movement in the 1960s came the beginnings of feminist theology. The purpose of feminist theology is not to deny males and declare that females are the best. The purpose is to use the anger that comes from feeling devalued to search for creative and alternative ways of understanding God and the world that will be more life giving to all of God's creation.

The tendency is to become afraid of the anger and to once again repress it, turning it into self-hatred, or to project it onto other women, saying that females who want to change the status quo are not real women, thus turning the anger into gender hatred. Either way results in hatred against females.

Sallie McFague, in my opinion, is one of many female theologians doing an excellent job of using anger in a creative manner. I chose her for several reasons. Her model of God follows the traditional trinitarian model. Her model is metaphorical; that is, she is not denying past metaphors of God but is offering other metaphors that she thinks will help us to understand our particular time in history. Finally, her model of God as Mother, Lover, and Friend values the best of being female and offers helpful metaphors for enabling females to value our devalued selves.

God as Mother values relationships, nurture, and creativity. Females are relational, nurturing, and creative. God has a personal relationship with humanity. God is not divorced from our feelings, needs, and wants. God is with us rather than being a distant ruler. At the same time, God as Mother, the upholder of justice, recognizes the purposefulness of anger when something is unjust and well-being and fulfillment are being blocked. Nurturer and just judge are not in opposition to each other but work together as partners to provide the best care possible to God's creation.

God as Mother places value on female connectedness with all the world and God's creation. Traditional theology has split God away from too close a connection with humanity and the world out of fear of diluting God's power and authority. If God is God, then God does not need to worry about losing power and authority.

God as Lover supports our need for being valued, for mutual recognition—I see and value you, and you see and value me. God cares passionately for all of humanity. God cares for and values females. God wants females to be seen and heard. God wants us as females to value ourselves. God as Lover supports our journey toward self-discovery, self-assertion, and ultimately self-worth. God knows that if I value myself, then I will value others and I will value God. We are bound together in an intimate relationship of worth.

God as Friend calls all of us to be companions with God and God's work. We are reminded that friendship is a relationship based on mutual trust and commitment. It is not a one-way street. Females in relationships have a tendency to give more than receive. Giving is important, but so is receiving. God does not intend for anyone to sacrifice the self, to be a martyr. God wants us to be trusting human beings, not masochists. This means trusting, sharing thoughts and feelings with spouses, children, friends, religious community, and others. Male and female are called to be advocates. A female is to be an advocate for herself and her value.

Traditional theology with God as Father supports the traditional gender roles with the husband and father as head of the household. These gender roles throughout the years created a separation with God in heaven and human beings on earth. These gender roles created a separation between the sexes so that males and females are rarely able to understand and trust each other. God as Mother, Lover, and Friend reminds us that God made human beings to be cocreators in God's work of love in the world. God made male and female in God's image to be helpmates for each other. We need strength, power, and protection as well as connection, nurture, and creative power. Both males and females are capable of being gifted in any of these abilities.

Being willing to entertain different images and models of God is important as I shift now to a chapter on abuse. Unfortunately, for many years the traditional theological models supported the denial and continuation of abuse. There is hope today in that new theological models and images are calling for us to become advocates against abuse.

5

The God I Worship Hurts Me

"I just don't understand why it hurts so much to go to church. Usually, personal prayer helps me to center myself and to find calm from the pain of the abuse. I feel ashamed sitting in the pew and wonder if everybody knows my father sexually abused me. Will God strike me dead because my skin crawls each time the minister prays to God the Father? I can't stand to hear 'God the Father.' I think of my father who abused me all those many years."

Through the story of Jill, this chapter examines the extremes in our culture of physical and sexual abuse and how male images of God cause abused women pain. For a woman who has experienced incest with a father, grandfather, uncle, cousin, or brother, the use of "Father," "Son," "our Brother, Jesus," and similar terms in worship often stirs up mixed feelings and shame related to the father or brother or male who violated the trust of the female. Many times Jill struggled with how to view God as Father without conjuring up the image of her human abusive father. She was raised as a Roman Catholic, and the image of Father was powerfully embedded in her psyche. Although in her head she knew that the two fathers were different, she could not separate the difference between Father and father because of the depth of betrayal.

Jill is a thirty-five-year-old divorced female whom I saw in therapy for two years. Her presenting issues were low self-esteem, difficulty in trusting relationships with men because of paternal incest, problems finding healthy relationships with men because of the sexual and physical abuse, and internal chaos from being raised by alcoholic parents. She is the third oldest of six siblings and the oldest female. Jill was sexually abused by her father from ages four through twelve; then he started abusing her younger sister. The ending of abuse coincided with the beginning of her menstrual cycle.

Because of drinking, her mother was neglectful and often in bed. Until Jill reached the age of ten, her paternal grandmother, who lived downstairs, helped to care for the family. Her father was the "nurturing" parent who tended to the children's basic needs. Jill was confused because he also sexually and physically abused her. She had little to no positive connection with either of her parents. Her connections were to her younger siblings, for whom she provided care, and to her grandmother.

Her grandmother treated her kindly but gave her the message that females were worth less than males. She could not survive in the world without a male. Her grandmother taught her the gender polarity that males are the dominant protectors and females are the self-sacrificing givers. It was confusing to her that her "protector father" abused her and her siblings and her "giving mother" lay in bed most of the time.

When Jill was sixteen, her father died, and soon afterward her mother married another alcoholic. Jill left home to be on her own. She put herself through college even though her family told her she would never finish. She met and married a man who turned out to be physically abusive. Unfortunately for Jill, love for her was tied up with abuse, neglect, and shame.

She struggled with leaving a physically abusive marriage because she feared God the Father would condemn her. Her religious upbringing intensified this belief. Her church did not believe in divorce and believed females were responsible for what their husbands did. Added to these beliefs were a grandmother and a father who believed divorce was a sin. Her mother had never divorced, even though her father was abusive. Through some inner strength, Jill made the decision to divorce; however, she continued to live with much guilt, shame, and fear that she had committed the ultimate sin. She feared love since the love she had known had been destructive.

Initial work centered on listening to her and helping her learn to calm herself inside. Because of her destructive fear of love, I worked patiently and intentionally with Jill. I was aware that too much closeness would frighten her but too much distance would feel like abandonment. Slowly, we talked about the sexual abuse and her feelings of unworthiness and shame. I supported her decision to go to an Al-Anon group and to find a sponsor. She went to meetings at least three times a week. The Al-Anon group was a lifeline for her. Jill found other women who were struggling with similar issues. She found an understanding community willing to talk about abuse, alcohol, and struggles to trust and love.

After six months of therapy, she said, "I know I need to love myself to love God. The problem is that loving myself seems not normal." Jill reminded me again of the interrelationship of self-image with God image. Her image of herself was dominated by the shame of incest and lack of mutual recognition. The feelings of shame were strong because the secret of sexual abuse in the family had been broken by one of her sisters. Despite the strong feelings of shame, Jill began to work on re-imaging herself as a person without shame, a person who is lovable and good. She borrowed from my ego strength to do this. We used the therapeutic space to struggle with her positive and negative self-images and to exorcise herself of the shameful and unlovable images of self.

Jill came to a place in her recovery where she wanted to feel angry about the abuse and neglect in her family, but she felt scared of her anger. Her anger might hurt someone. I recognized the depth of her fear and acknowledged this to her. We regularly discussed her fear. I assured her that her anger would not hurt me or another. Her anger would help her to free herself of her negative feelings and self-images. Through the use of her imagination, she fantasized the worst expression of her anger and constructive expressions of her anger.

Gradually, she began to express some of her anger with my holding much of her anger for her. Sometimes she felt overwhelmed by her anger and rage, but I provided a constant support and safe place for her to be with her anger. We talked about how God could handle her anger as well. She was not alone with her anger because God got angry at abuse.

Jill initially felt angry with her mother for being neglectful and not providing protection. Although her father violated her more than her mother did, it was important for Jill to address her issues with her mother first. Until she could deal with her anger at her mother, she remained bound to her mother because of the same-sex mother-daughter dynamic. As she began to separate from her mother and express her anger and sadness that her mother could not protect her from her father, she gained a more realistic picture of her mother. It freed Jill to begin to love herself. She became less dependent on taking care of others and more focused on caring for herself.

Again she used my ego strength, positive mirroring, and mutual recognition to explore more loving images of herself and her world. Having been dissatisfied in her work, she found a better position in the same company, applied for it, and got it. She began to learn that her choices for herself could lead to a positive impact on her world. Consequently, her self-esteem grew.

It was normal for Jill to follow a pattern of feeling good about herself and then finding ways to feel bad about herself. This is true for the change process that often goes two steps forward, one step backward. The person experiences clash and conflict with the old self system that does not want to change and the new self-image and self-esteem that are developing.

Jill found it scarier to consider re-imaging her relationship with her father. Although he was deceased, snapshots of him lived inside Jill. Her father had provided her with the illusion of safety and nurture. This illusion made it difficult for her to place the responsibility of the incest on her father. Jill felt that the situation was her fault and that she was bad inside. She was not worthy of love, particularly male love, and she was terrified of dating again. She used her fear to devalue herself and to confirm her internal ugliness. From me and from her Al-Anon group she heard different perspectives that laid the blame at her father's feet and said to her that she was good and lovable.

As she courageously continued to tell her painful story, she began having night terrors centered on the incest with her father. I listened and supported her. I supported her use of journaling. Journaling about the night terrors helped her to banish them by writing about her father and providing a safe, neutral space where she could deposit her terrors outside herself.

Eventually, she began to talk about her pain associated with going to church. Usually, prayer was a way for her to center herself back into her spirit. During this time of intense remembering, prayer seemed to lead her back to the shame of the sexual, physical, and emotional abuse. Although it was so painful to go to church that her intuition told her not to go, she asked me, "If I don't go to church, will God strike me dead?"

I supported her decision to take a break from church. This seemed important since she knew I was a minister and saw me as an authority figure. Together we explored her fear of God and its connection to her abusive father. Instead of church, she began going to a women's relationship group that was supportive and nurturing. At church she felt paranoid about what the other churchgoers would think if they knew she was abused. Church would become an option again after she worked through her intense fear and shame.

As we explored her pain about church, it became clear that her God was like her father, abusive and punitive. Intellectually, she knew that God could be other than male, but it was hard for her to imagine God in a different way. She was raised to believe God was Father and to honor her father. Honor your father and mother is one of the Ten Commandments. God as Mother was not helpful because her human mother was neglectful and manipulative.

At Al-Anon, God was the Higher Power, but this description of God seemed too impersonal to her. Jill wanted an image of God that was not attached to shame, abuse, and neglect and that was personal. The constant reminder in the traditional church of God as Father created too much pain for her. She did not have the ego strength to separate the two different concepts of father from each other. Her experience of her earthly father was so abusive (sexual, physical, and emotional) that she could not image God as a compassionate Father. Jill helped me to see more clearly the power of images of God to help or hinder self-development and self-esteem. On the positive side, she was searching for new, constructive images of God.

Psychologically, God as Father, in particular, and God as Mother activated the need for her to protect herself from shame and to be a loyal and obedient daughter who takes care of others first and herself last. Discovering a positive, constructive new image of God would provide a holding place to put her pain and shame without cutting herself off from herself or activating the old wounds. With this new image, she would be able to pray again and to have God's help in working through the continued pain of sexual abuse.

Through her positive, nurturing experiences with the Al-Anon and women's relationship groups, Jill began to conceive of God as a friendly spirit of community and love. The emphasis in her women's group on the body as good and worthy of loving helped her to begin working through years of secret shame associated with her body and soul. Her connection to her female group provided her with a caring community she had never experienced. There she continued the process of deconstructing her shame associated with her father and the punitive, abusive image of God as Father. She was able to believe in the group's care and concern and to delight in herself. Firmly in place with a caring community of people who understood her abuse, Jill ended therapy; she had come to a point of being able to image herself in more positive ways.

Jill's intense level of shame caused her to be sensitive to the church's ambivalence about sexual violence. Only in recent years has the church taken an active stance against sexual violence and other forms of abuse. Only in recent years have ministers been encouraged to report abuse and to educate congregations on the reality of abuse.

Many churches continue to deny that there is a problem with abuse. Many churches participate in blaming the victim with statements such as these: "This is a cross you must bear"; "Jesus said to 'turn the other cheek'"; "If you pray harder, he will quit abusing you"; "You must be getting punished for something you did wrong"; "He's a fine Christian man; you must be lying"; "Honor your father and mother"; "Spare the rod and spoil the child"; and "The father is head of the household; it is not up to us to interfere with his rule."

The statistics on sexual violence are alarming. It is known generally that one in four girls is at risk of child sexual abuse. Approximately 90 percent of abused children know their offender, who usually is a member of the family. Every two minutes a woman is raped. Every eighteen seconds a woman is beaten by a man she lives with. Every five minutes a child is molested. Every thirty minutes a daughter is molested by her father.[1] Abuse often goes on for years. Most abusers deny the abuse and will not stop abusing until caught and helped. Males commit the overwhelming majority of sexual violence and abuse. Why?

As I have indicated, in Western civilization gender polarity exists where male is dominant and female is submissive. Because of gender polarity, many men have a difficult time understanding what it is like to be assaulted sexually. Males grow up experiencing male privilege; they have virtually no knowledge of what it is like to be subordinate and devalued. Males spend a lot of energy not being female or anything associated with femaleness.

Some men do not comprehend that females are people, too, rather than objects to be used at will. The myth is that the dominant-submissive formula sparks erotic desire. Marie Fortune, a minister who founded and directs the Center for the Prevention of Sexual and Domestic Violence in Seattle, Washington, writes, "In our society, women and children fulfill the subordinate status necessary to complement male dominance and thus are vulnerable targets for exploitation and abuse."[2]

Traditional male sexuality is based on dominance versus relationship. It consists of the following elements. The sexual object must be "innocent," passive, and subordinate. A lack of regard for the other person as an autonomous individual leads to the ability to objectify and rationalize the experience. Males find it hard to believe that what they want often is not what females want. There is an unwillingness to accept responsibility for one's acts. A female is there to be used. There is the inability to find erotic and emotional pleasure with an equal. These elements lead to confusing healthy sexual activity with sexual violence.[3] It becomes difficult for people to understand that sexual abuse and rape have nothing to do with sex and everything to do with power, dominance, and violence.

The erroneous interpretation of the second and third chapters of Genesis, where the woman is created by God from man's rib to be a companion to man, leads to the misunderstanding that the female's role is first and foremost to serve man and meet man's needs. The creation story in Genesis 1, where man and woman are cocreated and coequal, has been downplayed in favor of the second creation story. Males believe they have the right to sexual access to almost any female.[4]

As an adolescent, I could not walk down the street without having some male make nasty, sexual remarks to me. At fourteen or forty, no woman wants to hear offensive sexual remarks. At the age of sixteen, while riding the Greyhound bus, I learned to defend myself from roving hands. I was fair game to any male. I still experience tremendous anger that we live in a culture permitting sexual abuse. For years I was told that if anything happened to me, it would be my fault because I was going places by myself without the protection of a male. The problem was that I knew too many females who followed all the proper rules for being a female and were molested and raped by those who were to protect them.

It made sense to me that my parents spent time teaching me how to protect myself from predators out in the world. Knowing how to protect oneself is important for everyone. However, I continue to wonder why men do not hold each other accountable for abuse and rape. What would our society be like if the males we knew said "no" to sexual exploitation and disciplined the men who abused women and children? What made absolutely no sense to me was child sexual abuse. Who could abuse a baby? What society do we live in that has condoned such behavior for years? Not all societies have rape and abuse.

A number of anthropological studies indicate that there are plenty of cultures where rape and abuse are virtually nonexistent. Societies that are prone to rape and abuse view females as subordinate objects to be dominated. Societies that are free of abuse and rape show respect to females as equals in culture and religion and often have a primary female deity or a male/female deity.[5]

All of this raises questions: Does God intend for sexual violence to occur particularly against women and children? Did God create females to be victims and males victimizers? If sexual violence is a part of the natural order, then women are created to be victims. If sexual violence is unnatural, then there is a very different answer; there is hope that changes can occur.

The Judeo-Christian tradition does not support sexual violence as natural. Instead, sexual violence is a form of sin. God created human beings to be in relationship with God and with each other. Through relationships, both redemption and sin occur. Rather than being rebellion against God, sin is any unnecessary violation of the well-being of any aspect of creation. Sin occurs when we freely choose to victimize another person. Sin occurs when we alienate ourselves from relationship with God and thus break right relations with other human beings. Marie Fortune writes, "Sin is the rupture of relationship and may be experienced psychologically, physically, spiritually, and socially."[6]

Because God created us as relational beings, the responsibility for both sin and redemption lies with God and humanity. How we relate or do not relate with each other contributes to redemption or sin. Redemption is the renewal of relationship with God, self, and others. Religious communities and society are responsible as well because no one lives in isolation from God's creation. How we value or devalue right relations determines to a great extent how fertile the soil is for sin and evils such as sexual violence.

What are right relations? Two important themes in the Bible are love and justice. God's understanding of love moves us to seek union with others and God even if the other is different. We are called to value and respect the other person as God's creation. God's love consists of give-and-take that does not include dominating behavior. God's love may move one to use anger to right a wrong and an injustice, but it is not a vengeful anger. God's understanding of justice calls for mutual and equal relations based on trust and respect, including bodily respect.[7]

Marie Fortune offers the following questions as guidelines for right relations: Do I have equal power in this relationship?

Do I respect the wishes of the other person and myself regarding intimacy and physical and sexual contact? Do I trust the other person not to betray or intentionally injure me? Do I freely choose to interact with this person? Does the other person freely choose to interact with me? If these questions can be answered positively, then there is the possibility for right relations to exist.[8]

In the case of parent-child, teacher-student, counselor-client, pastor-parishioner, or doctor-patient, it is the responsibility of the person in power and authority to respect the rights of the other person, to safeguard the other's welfare, and to not misuse power and authority. The person in power is to get his or her primary needs met through someone who can have an equal relationship. It is the responsibility of the community to provide checks and balances for parental and professional accountability.[9]

Theologically, sexual violence and abuse rupture the relationship with God, self, and community. They violate the person psychologically, physically, spiritually, and communally. They exploit another person's sacredness. They violate bodily integrity and relational and communal trust. The abused person may need years to regain trust. They distort and misuse healthy human sexuality and can cause future sexual problems. They violate the offender's selfhood in that God did not create us to be abusive.[10]

I believe it is important for all of us to recognize the depth of rupture so that we take seriously the need to re-image God and our traditional theology. Traditionally, the sin of sexual violence has been attributed to the victim rather than the offender.[11] Victimization was viewed as a sign of sinfulness in that "nothing bad happens to good Christians." Too often the church misunderstands sexual violence to be related to sex rather than an act of abusive domination and power. To the victim, sexual violence is not sex. Rather, it is disrespect of another's personhood and sacred worth.

Traditional patriarchal theology with God as Father is hierarchical. The hierarchical structure of traditional theology can enable people to misunderstand right relating. It contributes to the notion that God is in heaven and is taking care of all sin and evil. This notion lets humanity off the responsibility hook. Also, it contributes to the idea that human fathers are lords of their homes and are not accountable to the broader community. Whatever happens inside the family is private rather than public. I have no desire to make my private family life totally public, but I am responsible to the community for wrongdoing.

Sallie McFague's model of God as Mother, Lover, and Friend offers a relational and responsible understanding of God that would not tolerate sexual violence. Relational theology reminds us that we were created to justly love one another and are responsible with God for bringing about heaven on earth. Jill's re-imaging of God as a friendly spirit of community and love is supported by McFague's understanding of God as Friend. We are to be companions and advocates for each other and for God, enabling each other to achieve God-given potential. We are to respect and value each other enough that we listen and pay attention to each other's needs. Although these values of respect and relationship exist in traditional theology, they often are overridden by the need to make God the Father the all-powerful owner of the universe.

Jill, in particular, raises for the religious community the question: What happens when the God to whom one prays leads one back to the pain of the past? By having a place to explore her self-image and God image, Jill began a process of re-imaging God that led her to debunk the old, destructive images of God and self. More than any of my clients, Jill made me aware of the interrelationship of self-image and God images. My belief was confirmed that God images can be harmful. God images have a personal and a political impact.

6

Breathing New Life into Old God Images

"For the first time I heard a female voice in my dreams. I've never heard a female voice before in my dreams. Isn't that odd because I'm female. I'm glad and I feel strong hearing her, I mean my voice."

Later on the same woman went on to say she felt pulled to light candles to Mother God. Praying to the Goddess felt nurturing, and she needed nurture. She asked me if that was all right to do. I said, "Why not?" She set up a little altar in her bedroom. Because she had grown up in an Orthodox Jewish family that was extremely patriarchal, lighting candles to Mother God and listening to her female voice were radical changes. The changes would lead her to begin to claim her own voice and strength, which had a positive ripple effect on her entire life.

I did not suggest to her that she pray to Mother God. I did encourage her to wonder: Who is God for her? What kind of God would enable her to grow and change? What image of God would help her to love herself and others more? The therapeutic space provided the place for her to explore these questions and to imagine something different for her life. Without providing time and space for re-imaging it is difficult to breathe new life into old God images.

Imagination enables us as human beings to move beyond set belief and cultural structures. Imagination is thinking, feeling, and visualizing beyond one's set images and beliefs. Imagination enables us to access God's redemptive possibilities. Within historical existence there is God's lure of infinite possibilities. God's lure is the force and energy of love that is present every day in our lives, inviting and pulling us toward possibilities for change. With the help of God's redemptive presence the self that is stuck in seeing nothing beyond the old snapshots can choose new images to add to the photo album.

God's lure introduces novelty into set belief structures. God's redemptive presence encourages humanity to look beyond the ordered, traditional structures to different images that might be more freeing and transforming for all, particularly at certain periods of time in history. God's Spirit lives and breathes among us and is not static. Although God's redemptive lure is present, there is resistance to change set belief structures. God as Father and other patriarchal images of God are embedded in our religious communities, culture, and individual psyches. Theologian Rebecca Chopp writes, "Father is thus not only a metaphor but a law and an ordering."[1]

Because there is resistance to change, for re-imaging to occur we must be intentional about providing the time and space to work on changing set belief patterns and adding new snapshots to the photo album. The time and space can happen through a variety of mediums, such as therapy, groups, journaling, drawing, music, dance, a conversation partner, prayer, meditation, retreating, and worship, among others. What is important is the way that you can best provide time and space to work on liberating images of self and God.

The space enables you to be intentional about realizing there are set belief patterns and myths that resist change. It provides the place to discover these beliefs and patterns and to work on making way for the new images. The rest of this chapter will explore the purpose and use of space for re-imaging and will offer five steps for making constructive use of space.

A person and/or community can make many choices at any given time because of God's lure and infinite vision of possibilities. God attempts to encourage us to make choices that open doors to positive and constructive personal and social change. However, new images threaten the accepted order; thus, they may be experienced with fear and suspicion. There is a normal process of repeating the past. The refrains recur of "what was good for my parents is good for me" and "we have done it this way in our family, our church, our community for years."

The present inherits these feelings and beliefs from the past, so it is important to have a critical and disciplined analysis of the norms, traditions, and images from the past that operate in our present lives. Before room can be made for new images, we must be aware of the old images, and we must work through our resistance to change.

I have developed a five-step process that uncovers the past and prepares the way for allowing the imagining of new images in the present. I believe it is a lifelong process and we do not necessarily do the steps in order. The five steps are guides for the areas that need liberating if re-imaging is going to happen. I will use examples from my life and the lives of other clients presented in this book to illustrate the process.

Step One: Discovering the Self as a Female in Family, Culture, and Religion

The first step is discovering the self for females. Who am I? Who am I as a female? What is my image of God? Is my image of God a helpful or harmful image? Where did I learn my beliefs about self and God? What cultural and religious images and beliefs have I bought into?

At this step it is important to gain some understanding of your personal family, religious, and cultural backgrounds. These three areas offer immediate clues about what beliefs are internalized from the past. These beliefs need to be identified before re-imaging can occur.

Born in 1955, I grew up in a post–World War II environment that placed value on progress and prosperity. Consequently, I am part of the baby boom generation. During the war, women were in the workforce; after the war, there was a major shift in redefining gender roles. Although both of my parents went to college, my mother, who graduated as a registered nurse, did not work until I was sixteen. Instead, she raised babies, and my father worked as an engineer. I lived in the same house from age two until I left for college. I grew up in a time of stability, yet rigid role definitions. Men worked and made money. Women raised babies and took care of the home. Men were associated with the public arena and women with the private, emotional arena.

There were some deviations in my family in that my paternal grandmother worked as a schoolteacher until she married and my maternal grandmother worked her entire life. Both of them were products of the depression when work was a necessity for survival. I felt proud of my grandmother who worked. She was a role model for me.

As a white middle-class baby boomer, I grew up with certain gender role expectations. I was to marry and raise children. Since I was from an educated family, I was to receive a college education so that I could better educate my children and be an intelligent partner for my husband.

I was raised in the Presbyterian Church; until 1969 there were no ordained female ministers and then not many until the 1980s. The minister was a man. The elders of the church session were men. God was called "Father," "Lord," "Master," "King," and "Son," and there was no such thing as inclusive language. I did not hear of inclusive language until I entered seminary. God for me was Father, Son, and Holy Ghost, which was the trinitarian formula I learned at church. I learned that female church workers were missionaries, church-school teachers, and directors of Christian education. Women served the food and cleaned up at church suppers.

The snapshots in my internal photo album are of females being caregivers, child rearers, servers, and the emotional and practical supporters for males who went out into the world. I understood that men's work was more important than women's work. Men's work brought home a paycheck. I understood that males were in charge of the religious communities, although females often did much of the daily work. Men had the power and made the decisions. That was true at home as well. Although my mother kept the house running on a daily basis, my father made the major decisions. I learned that females were second-class citizens. Females were appreciated for all they did at the home but were not truly considered capable of making tough intellectual and moral decisions.

As I explored where these devaluing snapshots of being female came from, I discovered that I grew up in a historical time that was based on Freudian notions that females were disfigured males who were morally inferior to males. Because females were the weaker sex, they were not as capable of making moral decisions. We know today that female psychology is different from male psychology and that female decision making is different from but not less than male decision making.

In general, females value relationships more than males do, so females keep in mind the complex web of relationships when making decisions. Male decision making often appears more clear-cut because it does not take into account relationships as often as female decision making does. This we now know means that there are at least two different ways of making decisions that are valid rather than one being better than the other. In the pluralistic world in which we live with many cultures represented, we know that there are a number of ways different people and cultures make decisions and there are different sets of values and morals as well.

In my research I have learned that because of the structure of gender polarity that views male as dominant and female as subordinate, anything that is different from male is considered less than male. This structure still is in place, but it is in transition. I believe gender polarity is one of the reasons there is backlash in our culture against diversity in our country and world. Diversity threatens the structure of gender polarity and appears to threaten the male power base. The reality is that when relationships are viewed mutually instead of one up and one down, there is plenty of love and power for all.

Step Two: Allowing the Female Self to Be Angry without Guilt

I can guarantee that once you identify the beliefs you inherited from your family, culture, and religion that exist in your self photo album, you are going to feel angry with the images that devalue you and hinder your self-discovery and self-assertion. As I wrote earlier, anger gives you the energy to say that something is not all right, to say "no," to say, "I need to change," or "Something in my life needs to change."

Sue is close in age to me. When she realized that she really was a maid for her husband and sons, she got angry. Why couldn't they help around the house? They were strong and able-bodied. She ran the house and worked forty hours a week. We no longer live in the post–World War II era where families have the luxury of only one adult in the workforce. Most families need two incomes. Sue was exhausted and suicidal because she had no energy or room for herself. Once she identified part of the problem, she was able to constructively use her anger to empower her to say to her husband and sons, "I need your help, and you are going to help me if you love me."

Fortunately for Sue, her family did love her and agreed to help. They were going along with the way in which they had been programmed and were quite willing to pitch in to help her when they were made aware of her need. Often we hope that others will see our need and respond without being asked. Others noticing our need rarely happens. If you want something to change, you are going to have to ask for help and change.

This is a time of clash and conflict between the old images and the new images that are forming. There will be resistance to change. Guilt over anger is a form of resistance for females. Since we are taught that it is not female-like to consider our own needs when we get angry and consider our own needs, guilt usually appears. Like Gail, who was afraid to express anger at the boyfriend who dumped her, many of us disguise guilt as fear of hurting another person's feelings if we express our anger.

In the course of living in relationship we all are from time to time going to hurt each other's feelings. The hurt feelings usually go away when people are able to share with each other what was going on. As human beings, we are created to be able to withstand a certain amount of hurt and disappointment. A part of healthy relating is talking with each other about hurt feelings and disappointments so that we can clear the air. Real guilt is reserved for true hurt where a law or moral is broken. If I lie, cheat, or steal, I hope I feel guilty. If I tell someone I am going to do something and then I do not, I should feel guilty. But sharing anger with someone about something not being all right is not grounds for guilt, even if the person gets hurt feelings.

When May, our divorced professional woman, began to realize that sexism existed at work, at home, and in her church and culture, she felt angry. It dawned on her that her mother never learned to drive a car; she remained very dependent on her father and on May. May was angry that there was no one for her to depend on when she was growing up. Her anger helped her to understand that, on the one hand, she learned to be very independent, but on the other hand, she had major dependency needs that kept pulling her down because she was afraid to get them met. Her anger helped her to see that it was important for her to find others she could depend on.

Jill, who was sexually abused by her father, felt angry at the church for using "God the Father" so much and not using inclusive language. She felt angry that because of the church's ambivalence toward abuse, she felt shame when she went to church. Was it okay to feel angry at God for allowing abuse? Realizing that God could handle her anger freed Jill to consider other avenues where she could get her spiritual needs met. Maybe at a later time she could find a church that used inclusive language. Since at this time it stirred up too many feelings of shame to go to church, having a women's spirituality group was a great alternative.

For all of these women it was important to get angry and then be able to move forward in a new direction. With their anger they could say that everything was not okay. The anger provided energy to explore and discover where the old beliefs came from and to search for new ways to assert oneself in the world.

Step Three: Focusing on the Female Voice and Experience

Most of us have grown up in a world dominated by male images, voices, and experiences. When someone asks you to name a hero, who do you think of first, a male or a female? Generally, most of us think of a male hero first. Even though gender images and roles are changing and there is more respect for female ability, women have a long way to go. Nightly, thousands of fans go to see men play baseball, football, and basketball. Although it was something to celebrate that more than ninety thousand fans went to watch the U.S. women's soccer team win the 1999 World Cup, this is only the beginning for females. It was one event for females whereas males have many such events. In a country that says we do not need an Equal Rights Amendment because females have equal rights, women make twenty to twenty-five cents less per dollar than men. Females' value is increasing, but it is not yet equal with males' value.

To counter the devaluing in our culture, women must focus on valuing femaleness. Focusing on valuing oneself as a woman is a way of recognizing femaleness. Without positive recognition, the self will continue to devalue itself and to focus more on the negative than the positive. When my client May said that she heard a female voice in her dream for the first time, it was a day to celebrate. She was beginning to value all of herself as important.

In my journey I began the process of valuing the female voice and experience by learning more about my grandmothers. Both of my grandmothers had been strong and independent in their own ways. When my maternal grandmother lost everything in the depression, she picked up her five children, moved to the city, and found a job when few were finding work. I am told that she was the first female to work for the Internal Revenue Service in the state of Virginia. She worked until she retired and raised her family as well.

My paternal grandmother was one of nine children being raised in the mountains of Virginia, but she did not want to stay in the mountains. She managed to escape by going to a teachers' college and then teaching school in one-room schoolhouses until she met my grandfather. Her dream was to live a refined life in the city, and she accomplished her dream. When I was struggling with whether to go to a college near my family or accept a scholarship to a school far away, she was the one who said, "Go. Go where you want to go. Your parents will be okay." Her voice helped me to follow my dream.

Both of my grandmothers used their dreams to create new images of how life could be for them and for their families.

Neither one accepted her lot in life as how life had to be. They used their dreams and imaginations to find a more satisfying life. They used their faith in new possibilities as energy to fuel moving into new cities, jobs, and adventures. If my maternal grandmother had not explored new snapshots for her life, she would have remained in the country with her five children living an impoverished life. My paternal grandmother would have remained in the mountains and become a bitter woman who could never be satisfied with where she lived.

Next, I spent time looking at my relationship with my mother in a different light. For years I judged my mother by male standards, and she fell short because she was female, not male. When I began to understand what it means to be female in our family and culture, I viewed her life differently. I was freed to value her for who she is rather than for who I wanted her to be. I was able to recognize her love and strength, which she had poured into me. When an opportunity arose for me to go to college away from home, she was the one who made me fill out the application. For years, I thought she was the one holding me back. Obviously, she was not holding me back. The devalued images of femaleness that came from culture, religion, and family, which I had internalized, were holding me back.

In seminary, I focused on the females in the Bible. Not until then did I know that there are so many strong female characters in the Bible—Rachel, Sarah, Abigail, Deborah, Tamar, Ruth, Naomi, Mary, Martha, Priscilla, and others. My interest in them was aroused during my first year of seminary after a female professor told the story of the daughters of Zelophehad (Num. 27).

Zelophehad, who was deceased, had no sons. At that time property was passed from father to son. The daughters of Zelophehad went to Moses and asked him to talk to God about allowing their father's property to be passed on to them. Without Zelophehad's property the women were going to be homeless. In an unusual move, Moses took the daughters' request to God, and God told Moses to write a new statute and ordinance passing a father's inheritance to his daughters if he had no sons.

In Numbers 36 this statute is refined in that a daughter is to marry inside the father's tribe. If the daughter marries outside the tribe, then the property is to remain within the tribe. However, daughters could still keep their father's property if they remained within the tribe. This statute was a revolutionary shift for the people of Israel, and the change would not have happened if Zelophehad's daughters had not decided to challenge the tradition and to imagine that life could be different and more fair. Numbers 36 has been used in modern courts of law to uphold the passing of property to females when there have been no sons and other male family members have wanted to take the property away from the daughters.

The professor's sharing of this biblical story opened a new world to me. Having grown up surrounded by male biblical images—Jesus, the twelve disciples, Moses, Abraham, Joseph, Jacob, and Paul—I did not realize that there are strong female images in the Bible. From that point I began a personal search of the female characters and images in the Bible; each has her own unique story waiting to be discovered and explored. In 1976 when I started seminary, there were only a few books on women in the Bible. Today, there are many books on the subject that can help you in your exploration.

At seminary I was also introduced to inclusive language. The purpose of inclusive language is to avoid using any images of God that limit or disallow a certain group of people. The traditional trinitarian formula of Father, Son, and Holy Spirit became for me in inclusive language Creator, Redeemer, and Sustainer. Using nongendered and descriptive images of God helped me to deconstruct the male images of God embedded in my psyche. We cannot grow up in our society without having male images of God in our photo albums. Doing this allowed me to ponder more broadly the nature of God. Who was God for me?

A result of deconstructing the male images of God inside myself was that I felt a need not to use any male images at all. As a therapist, I know that any minority or oppressed group goes through a process of coming to terms with the oppression. At first, there is denial of the existence of any problems. Next, there is an inkling that maybe there is some truth to the reality of oppression. Then follows the realization that one is oppressed and anger about being a minority. To help move out of the oppression and anger, the next step is embracing oneself as okay as one is. It is a time of being proud, of exploring what it means to be female or African American or Jewish or disabled. Next come acceptance of who one is and recognition of being of worth as one is, even if the world does not recognize one's value. Finally, there is the ability to rejoin the community and to use a mixture of images while working for long-term change.

When I encountered my anger at the church and society for being sexist, I could no longer pray to "our Father" in the Lord's Prayer. I would skip over the "our Father" and substitute in my mind "our Mother." Today, I can pray to "our Father," although it is not my preferred prayer. The anger and the shift to inclusive language caused me to consider theologies that are more inclusive and mutual toward females and other minorities.

Upon graduation from seminary, I worked for six years as an associate pastor. I feel very fortunate that I worked with a senior pastor who believed in using inclusive language in worship. Many people came to appreciate the message of God's equality for all that was portrayed by our actions. It was not until I was working in the parish that I began to read biblical and theological feminist scholars who opened up another world for me. The purpose of the feminist scholars was not to displace males but to recognize and validate the lives and impact of females from the beginning of God's creation.

Throughout the last decade, I have read and celebrated women's wisdom, art, literature, religion, science, and sports. I went through a phase of reading only women authors to make myself discover the world of wonderful women authors. I would go to see only women's art exhibits and buy only music by women. I started playing soccer on a women's age thirty and over league. For several years I participated in a women's house church; a dedicated group of females who met monthly to explore different ways to use female rituals and images of God in worship.

In my personal therapeutic process where I was learning to discover, value, own, and assert myself, I re-imaged my trinitarian formula of Creator, Redeemer, and Sustainer to Amazon Woman, Blue Woman, and Spider Woman. Amazon Woman was to remind me that I am strong and capable of being a leader

of all people. I am competent. Blue Woman represented the part
of me that was nurturing. I needed not only to have compassion
for others but also to be caring and nurturing toward myself.
Spider Woman with her many webs reminded me that we are
created as relational beings. We are not isolated individuals, and
we do best when we work together for the good of each other
and for the good of community. Spider Woman challenges me to
receive from community as well as give.

In the last several years I have been praying to
Mother/Father God and/or to God and Goddess. I recognize
that we need each other, males and females, and that we bring
different perspectives to the world. Mothers and fathers, females
and males, need to be involved equally in child rearing. When
we honor, respect, and accept each other as equals, we are able
to relate more fully. I also continue to create new images for God
that support where I am in my spiritual and emotional journey.

Step Four: Placing Oneself in a Space
Where Feelings and Needs for Changing Self-Images
and God Images Are Respected and Validated

Persons to whom you are closest will resist change. Spouse,
partner, children, family members, friends, religious community
contacts, and others may not appreciate your journey and need
to re-image yourself, much less re-image God. The prevailing
view may be that God is sacred and is not to be touched. As you
take steps on your journey of self-discovery and self-assertion,
you will need support from others who understand your re-imaging
process. Without the support of others it will be much more
difficult to grow and change, and the chances of being overcome
by resistance and giving in to status quo will be much greater.

To re-image, we as human beings need a transitional space.
A transitional space is any type of space that mediates between
the inner psychic world and the outer world, between old and
new images and beliefs, and between individual self and culture.
Within transitional space, we suspend our set beliefs and images,
and we attempt to be open to new possibilities. It is a neutral
space where no judgments of right or wrong are made. It is a
place for exploration and openness to creativity. It is a place

where we are confronted with newness and often with challenge. Without the experience of transitional space, we cannot become selves.

Nature, culture, religion, and therapy can act as transitional spaces. Some cultural groups send their members on coming-of-age journeys or vision quests. Often, though, it is a quest only for males. Females, too, need to provide themselves with opportunities for quests and adventures. You do not have to go off into the wilds, but you do have to give yourself space so that you are not distracted by daily life and responsibilities for others. It is a time to be stripped of what is known and become open to new possibilities. It is a time to discover your gifts, abilities, and strengths. It might be going to a retreat center by yourself or taking a solo trip somewhere. Spending time alone in the car can be a form of transitional space.

Periodically, I go on a solo backpacking trip into the wilderness. The purpose of the trip is to take time and space to reflect on and reevaluate my life, to be open to new images and possibilities for my life. I have found throughout the years that unless I give myself some quiet space away from everything and everyone, it is difficult to hear God's word for me.

The six and a half years I was in psychoanalysis offered a type of transitional space for me. Lying on the couch and freely associating about whatever came to mind or whatever I felt permitted me to take space to hear my inner self that usually is drowned out by the noise of daily living. I hope that I provide my clients in pastoral counseling a space where they can safely open up to both the painful and the possible aspects of themselves.

The ritual space of religion and the therapeutic space of counseling are often called transitional spaces. For transitional space to be truly transitional, the person must be able to explore without judgment, to say "yes" and "no," and to come and go in the process of deconstructing and reconstructing set beliefs and images. For May, Sue, Gail, and Jill, pastoral counseling provided them with a transitional space.

May was able to explore the idea of equal images of God as female and male and to begin praying to God as Mother. Sue was able to say "yes" to herself and "no" to her husband and expand her image of God to include angel wings growing out of her back. Gail was able to become angry at God and know that God was not going to condemn her. Jill was able to find a women's spirituality group that allowed her to explore nurturing images of God for her and to find understanding in her struggle with the mainline church.

Support and space come in all shapes and sizes. I remember that my mother got up early most mornings to pray and read the Bible. She was giving herself a little bit of space before her busy day began. Taking a quiet, solo walk is a way to take space. Bible study, prayer, and meditation are helpful. Many women find regular retreats or spiritual pilgrimages sources of inspiration and change. Being a part of a women's Bible study group, a women's spirituality group, a women's support group, or a women's therapy group is a way to find transitional space and support.

Since women so often defer to men when in the company of men, and women need to have the space to explore freely who they are outside men, I believe it is important for space and support initially to be with females only. When you are more sure of your journey, it is fine to join mixed groups. For liberating images of God, the focus will need to be on yourself as a female. Know that there will likely be resistance to women's only space. Remember that the cultural and religious structure of gender polarity will attempt to convince you that women's only space is wrong or selfish or discriminatory.

We females rarely allow ourselves time and space. We usually are tending to others' needs. To re-image self and God, we need space and support. An ongoing challenge for me is not to give too much of myself away. I give too much of myself away when I ignore my need for space to listen to my inner self and to God's word for me. My current challenge is to remember that I cannot be of service to others if I ignore my own sacred space and self because I will run out of fuel and will burn out.

On my latest backpacking trip, the image of Eagle Woman came to me. In fact, I saw two eagles the first day I was out in the wilderness. Eagle Woman challenges me to continue to work to be free of my need to take care of others at the expense of myself. The eagle is very protective of her young, so she challenges me to be protective of myself. The eagle has keen vision, so she challenges me to have clarity of vision and purpose, to trust my intuition and not let my self-doubts confuse me. Her soaring spirit challenges me to soar with wings like eagles and to remember that I cannot do anything unless I take time to tend to my spirit. Strength will come to me through tending to my spirit, trusting in my clarity of vision, and protecting myself as I grow as a female child of God. God is able to interact with our spirits in transitional space. By envisioning new possibilities, we transcend the norm and open ourselves to God's presence in the world.

Step Five: Exploring Information, Theories, Theology, Myths, Imagination, and Conversation About Re-Imaging God

Step three was a more personal exploration of oneself as a female. Step five explores the wider and broader conversation about being female in today's world. What do psychology, sociology, theology, mythology, anthropology, and biology have to say about who females are? My hope is that this book has given you some glimpses into the richness of information available about being female. Because each one of us is a unique creation of God, each of us must do her own exploration to tailor the information to her needs, story, and photo albums.

I am writing from the perspective of a middle-aged, middle-class, white, Protestant, southern, highly educated woman. If you are Hispanic, African American, Korean, Jewish, Catholic, Muslim, or Hindu, you will have places where you differ because of your culture and your experience. Here in step five, we integrate our personal experiences of being female with a broader conversation with the world. In step five, we are reminded that we live in a diverse world and community. What can we learn from sisters different from us, and what can they learn from us? How can we be of support to each other?

There is no one way of being or doing. Beyond each one of us as a unique creation, there are many cultures. There are two genders, male and female. We are younger, middle-aged, and older adults. To be open to God's diverse creation, we must be open to difference. Difference will challenge us to grow and change. Difference will offer us new images and perspectives to integrate into ourselves.

God constantly challenges us to engage in a broader conversation than the one we know and are comfortable with. It is too easy to make assumptions unless we are open to newness. During this past year, I have begun work as a hospital chaplain. I have assumed that since I am an oppressed female, this is a place I can join together with my African American colleagues. What I have learned this year is that because I am white, others are suspicious of me and experience pain in relation to me. Because of cultural racism, I am perceived as more privileged than they, although I, too, have been oppressed.

This experience reminds me not to make assumptions. It also helps me to understand the resistance many males experience in allowing females space and believing that females need space. Many males do not perceive themselves as privileged or oppressors. What is important is to listen to how others perceive us. If I am perceived as being more privileged and powerful because I am white, then I need to take heed and learn to accept that this is reality. Then I need to have a conversation with my colleagues in as open a way as possible so that I might learn and grow. I need to expand my horizons to learn about the African American female experience.

In the same manner, each of us as a female is challenged to learn as much as she can about herself. The more I learn about myself and my relation to the broader world, the more I will be open to conversing with those who are different from me and the more I will be open to re-imaging. I have to re-image my intrapsychic self, and I have to re-image my cultural and religious self. Re-imaging myself will impact cultural and religious re-imaging. Re-imaging culture will impact re-imaging myself and leads to liberation.

A key piece in the whole process of re-imaging involves the images of God. I believe that our God images mediate between our individual and cultural selves. Therefore, God images hold a tremendous amount of power over us. Robert Coles, in his book *The Spiritual Life of Children*, invited 293 children to draw pictures of God. Of the 293 faces of God that were drawn, 255 were male faces. Patricia Reilly writes, "We leave childhood with the face of a male God permanently imprinted on our memory."[2] The male face of God that is imprinted on my memory is the face of a long haired, bearded white man.

To be able to re-image ourselves as well as re-image our culture so that we might be open to the diversity of the world, we have to re-image God. We have to learn as much as we can about the impact of God images on us as females. We have to challenge not only ourselves but also our religious communities to take responsibility for how traditional God images help or hinder personal growth and relationships with others who are different.

7

Practical Exercises
for Liberating Images of
God for Women

The most ancient image for the Divine was female. That female divine image is twenty-five thousand years old. It is the image of the Goddess.[1] The Egyptians, Greeks, Romans, Africans, Polynesians, Aztecs, American Indians, Hindus, Celts, Teutonic people, and many other cultures and peoples had divine images of God that were male and female. Predominantly the Judeo-Christian and Islamic heritages worship a male God only. Even within Islam there are ninety-nine descriptive names for Allah. It seems to me that it is now time in Western culture to come up with at least ninety-nine names for our Judeo-Christian God that include at least fifty female names for God.

To help you on your way to at least fifty female names for God, I leave you with the following female names for God to stimulate your imagination. Some of these names have their roots in the Judeo-Christian tradition; other names you will recognize from Greek or Roman myths and from American Indian tradition; and some names come from my imagination: Woman God, Queen of Heaven, Mother God, Sophia, El Shaddai

88

(Many-Breasted God), Womb of Compassion, Athena, Demeter, Aphrodite, Artemis, Pele, Isis, Asherah, Danu, Great Mother, Hecate, Persephone, Changing Woman, Grandmother, Divine Feminine, Midwife, Mother Bear, Faithful Mother, Goddess, Gaia, Shekinah (She Who Dwells Within), Eagle Woman, Nursing Mother, Comforting Mother, Laboring Woman, Mother Hen, Spider Woman, Warrior Woman, Amazon Woman, Female Spirit, Sister God, Grandmother Earth, Moon Woman, Snake Goddess, and Goddess.

Through six and a half years of experience in my personal therapy and ten years of experience as a pastoral counselor, I continue to discover that images provide a way of connecting the external reality of the world (religion, culture, family values) with the internal reality of the person's self (personal beliefs, values, and spirituality). Human beings think imaginatively about images. They are individual mental pictures and exist in relationship to the psyche, the world, the community, and God. Images provide a way to communicate a person's experience both outwardly to the world and inwardly to the self.

The imagination's power lies in enabling a person to connect images with words and experience and words and experience with images. Words, for the most part, are what we use to describe our experience, but they do not create the reality of experience itself. When this connection occurs, a person says, "Wow, that's it!" or the world says, "Now I understand." Confusion and conflict can occur when past and/or present images do not connect with a person's experience. Imagination becomes a way for a person to search for images that can connect with the experience.

There are several layers to making use of images. On an everyday level, we use images to name objects that are generally accepted, such as man, woman, tree, and flower. We use images to describe experiences of things we symbolize but cannot see, such as God, spirit, freedom, love, and justice. To come up with new images, we often will combine, reconstruct, deconstruct, or re-image several images. For example, when the typewriter was invented, the word "typewriter" was created out of "writing" and "typing." To describe the current computer age, new words have been created, such as "Y2K compatible." Our language is always in a process of adding new words that were created through the use of imagination.

I believe that God gave us the capacity to imagine as a way to continually offer new possibilities to our set beliefs and traditions. New images of God and new ways of being in relationship with each other as human beings can be created. The traditions of the past and present will attempt to prevent us from using our imaginations. Traditions provide security and stability, which are important. As human beings, we often choose conformity and repetition of the past over change and newness. How much power is held by images from the past determines how resistant a person is to adding new images to his or her internal photo album. At the same time, new images that come to us from God offer a breath of fresh air and encourage changes in self, religion, and society.

To help you in your re-imaging journey, I have placed within five categories a number of questions and exercises for guiding the re-imaging process. You may want to keep a notebook or journal with your answers to the questions and exercises. What I offer is only a beginning. There are plenty of other questions and exercises in the world to be discovered.

Childhood Images of God

1. From whom did you first hear about God? Was God spoken about in male or female pronouns and descriptions?
2. What was your childhood understanding of religion?
3. What names were used for God when you were a child?
4. What images of God were used in your religious community?
5. What was your image of God?
6. Was the religious authority of your childhood (pastor, priest, rabbi) male or female? Or did you have both a male and a female in authority?
7. Did your image of God grow and change as you grew and changed as a child? At what age did you adopt your predominant image of God?
8. How would you have liked to learn about God?
9. As a child, what images of God would have been helpful to you?

Relationship with Mother and Father

1. What traditional female roles did your mother follow? Which of these do you follow?
2. Were you ever aware that your mother was valued less than your father by the world?
3. What traditional roles did your father follow?
4. Were you ever aware that your father felt you were not equal to males?
5. Were you ever aware that you were valued less than males?
6. How did the traditional gender roles help or hinder your self-development? Did the traditional gender roles help or hinder how you imagined your future to be?
7. Did your parents encourage you as a female to get an education and have a career, or did they encourage you to marry?
8. Did you learn from your mother and father to defer to men?
9. As a young female, did you learn from your family to fear violence from males—sexual harassment, rape, physical abuse, etc.? How does this fear affect you today? What does your religious community do to prevent sexual violence?

Uncovering Old God Images

1. Pay attention to how often God is referred to in male terms in what you read and in prayers people say and how God is imaged at your religious services. Is God ever referred to in female terms or through the use of inclusive language? If not, why?
2. If you find resistance to re-imaging the male God, start a conversation with your inner resistant voice. Ask it: How can I be open to explore my religious past? Ask it: What is wrong with imaging God in female images?
3. Although you may not think of God in male or female terms, when you do use gendered images and pronouns, are they male or female?
4. Who were your saviors and heroes? Were any of them female?
5. Who are your favorite religious characters? Are any of them female?
6. What images, positive and negative, arise for you when you read the word "Goddess"? What were you taught about Goddess?

7. What images, positive and negative, arise for you when you read "God the Father"?
8. Write a letter to God the Father. Write a letter to God the Mother. What feelings and differences arise between the two?

Re-Imaging God as Female

1. Imagine God as female. What images arise? Write down as many female images of God as possible.
2. Suppose Jesus or Buddha or Muhammad was female. Would that make a difference for you? If so, in what way?
3. Reflect on these images of God: Queen of Heaven, Woman God, Mother God, Sophia, Many-Breasted God, She Who Dwells Within, Spider Woman, and Eagle Woman. What comes to your mind?
4. In what female ways has God spoken to you—a female voice, a wise woman who appears in a dream, the presence of a female spirit? What was this experience like for you?
5. Does it make a difference to you to know that the Bible describes God in female terms? In Exodus 19:4 God is a mother eagle; in Isaiah 42:14 God is a woman in labor; in Isaiah 49:15 God is an attentive mother; in Hosea 13:8 God is a mother bear; in Matthew 23:37 Jesus is a hen gathering her chicks; and in Luke 15:8–10 God is a woman searching for what is lost. What does it mean to you that God is described in the Bible in female images? Do any of these images resonate with you?
6. List all the devaluing images of femaleness that live inside you. Write down the positive image opposite the negative image. For example, for weak, write strong. What female God images would help you to overcome these negative images of yourself? Write down these God images, and use them in your daily prayer and/or meditation time. Use the positive female God images to help you affirm yourself.
7. If you are Christian, re-image the Trinity in female images.
8. In traditional prayers that use male images for God, substitute female images. For example, instead of praying "our Father who art in heaven," pray "our Mother." Pray these prayers

with female images on a regular basis for several months. Does re-imaging the traditional prayers make a difference for you?

9. Write your own prayers to the Goddess or female image of God of choice that you pray on a regular basis. What does it feel like to pray to a female God? Does it make a difference to your image of self?

10. For three months use only female pronouns and images for God. What thoughts and feelings are stirred up for you by this exercise? As the days go by, do you find yourself changing any? What is your experience with this exercise? Keep a journal of your experience.

11. Find another woman or a group of women who are re-imaging God as female, and receive support and creative ideas from the group.

Mutual Images of God

1. Examples of mutual God images are God and Goddess, God and Gaia, Father and Mother God, Brother and Sister God, Grandfather and Grandmother God, Grandfather Sky and Grandmother Earth, Sun and Moon, First Man and First Woman. What other mutual God images can you imagine?

2. What differences do you experience praying to God and Goddess or Mother and Father God rather than to Father God or Mother God?

3. Does praying to mutual God images help you respect the other gender more?

4. Does praying to other cultural images of God, such as Grandmother Earth and Grandfather Sky, help you to be more open to the diversity of the worldwide community of God?

It is clear to me that our religious communities and culture will not tolerate a sole female image of God. At the same time, a sole male image of God hinders the self-development of many females. In envisioning a mutual male/female God, the hope is that equal value will be placed on both males and females. Then I believe equality will become structured into individuals, religious communities, and culture.

For females to work through devaluing images and snapshots of femaleness, they will have to go through a phase of focusing on being female and putting female in first place. This includes imaging God through female images because male God images can work to devalue the image of being female. When females are allowed to freely develop a self, they can allow their children and others to freely develop and separate. Females will not have to defer to males to feel of worth and to have power in the eyes of society.

If mothers are not experienced as persons to dominate because they are different and less than males, then males will not need to devalue their mothers or other females to feel of value. Males can then be open to being nurturing and sensitive. Males will then be less threatened by being associated with femaleness. I believe then that males and females will be more open to female images of God.

Mutual relations between the sexes allow each person, whether male or female, to be capable of recognizing the other person as a helpmate rather than as an other to control, dominate, and fear. Male and female mutual images of God are necessary for mutual relations to occur between the sexes because images of God are embedded in our psyches and influence who we understand each other to be.

Conclusion

I sometimes wonder whether I am a female Don Quixote who is attacking windmills. For many, suggesting that God needs to be re-imaged is heresy. The simple answer is that God intended for the world to be patriarchal. God intended for males to be heads of household. If I would quit attacking windmills, then I could settle down and be a proper lady. What I know through personal experience, experience of the world, and knowledge is that God is a living God. As a living God, God grows and changes, offering to humanity new ways of being in relationship with God and with each other. My hope is that these new ways of being in relationship offer love and justice to each other.

As I have re-imaged God in female images, I have felt myself grow in self-esteem and value. In my work with my clients I have seen many women grow in self-worth and strength. By beginning to believe that females are equal to males, May was freed to be less dependent on males for worth and value, and she could begin to accept her strength and abilities. For Sue, by learning it is normal to say "no" to males and "yes" to herself, she began to find herself and grow again. Her depression lifted so that she could relate with those she loved.

Gail learned to no longer center her life on men and to get angry when she needed to. She was no less a Christian if she got angry. Allowing herself to get angry provided room inside herself to get on with her life and not continue to be weighed down by the past. Jill came to realize that she did not have to bear the blame and shame for her father sexually abusing her. She could believe that there is a loving community spirit present in society that is embracing and accepting her with both her gifts and her woundedness.

It is clear to me that God images mediate between cultural beliefs and individual personal beliefs. God created us as relational beings who live in community; self, religion, and culture are interrelated. For change to occur, the devaluing images of femaleness in culture, religion, and self must be re-imaged. Re-imaging the self will influence culture, and re-imaging culture will influence the self. The result of re-imaging is liberation.

I hope that I do not become like the Don Quixote of history who eventually came to his senses, succumbed to reality, and quit chasing windmills. I pray daily that God is fair to all, that a female's image of God encourages her to say "no," that a person's image of God does not lead to depression, that the image of God makes room for anger, and that the God who is worshiped provides solace, not hurt, to those who are abused. I hope that I remain passionately open to God's new possibilities so that new life might be breathed into old God images. In particular, at this point in history, I pray that room and acceptance will be made for female images of God.

Notes

Introduction

1. Anne Wilson Schaef, *Women's Reality: An Emerging Female System in a White Male Society* (San Francisco: Harper & Row, 1981), 27.

2. Patricia Lynn Reilly, *A God Who Looks Like Me: Discovering a Woman-Affirming Spirituality* (New York: Ballantine Books, 1995), 82.

1. Self-Image and God Image

1. Althea J. Horner, *Psychoanalytic Object Relations Theory* (Northvale, N.J.: Jason Aronson, 1991), 94–99.

2. Jill Savege Scharff and David E. Scharff, *Scharff Notes: A Primer of Object Relations Therapy* (Northvale, N.J.: Jason Aronson, 1992), 93.

3. Ana-Maria Rizzuto, *The Birth of the Living God: A Psychoanalytic Study* (Chicago: University of Chicago Press, 1979), 7.

4. Ibid., 44.

5. Ibid., 194.

6. Ibid., 196.

7. Ibid., 197.

8. Ibid., 197.

9. Ibid., 198.

10. Ibid., 200–201.

11. Ibid., 200.

12. Phyllis Trible, *God and the Rhetoric of Sexuality* (Philadelphia: Fortress Press, 1978), 18.

13. Barbara J. MacHaffie, *Her Story: Women in Christian Tradition* (Philadelphia: Fortress Press, 1986), 12.

2. The God I Worship Is Not Fair to Me

1. Rosemary Radford Ruether quoted in *Weaving the Visions: New Patterns in Feminist Spirituality*, ed. Judith Plaskow and Carol P. Christ (San Francisco: Harper & Row, 1989), 151.

2. MacHaffie, *Her Story*, 9.

3. Ibid., 7.

4. Ibid., 8.

5. Ibid., 18–19.

6. Bernard Meland, *Fallible Forms and Symbols: Discourses on Method in a Theology of Culture* (Philadelphia: Fortress Press, 1976), 122.

7. Doris Bernstein, *Female Identity Conflict in Clinical Practice* (Northvale, N.J.: Jason Aronson, 1993), 1, 18.

8. Jessica Benjamin, *The Bonds of Love: Psychoanalysis, Feminism, and the Problem of Domination* (New York: Pantheon, 1988), 23.

9. Carroll Saussy, *God Images and Self-Esteem: Empowering Women in a Patriarchal Society* (Louisville: Westminster/John Knox Press, 1991), 32–33.

10. Sue Monk Kidd, *The Dance of the Dissident Daughter: A Woman's Journey from Christian Tradition to the Sacred Feminine* (San Francisco: HarperSanFrancisco, 1996), 20.

11. Frank S. Pittman III, *Man Enough: Fathers, Sons, and the Search for Masculinity* (New York: Berkley Publishing Group, 1993), 276.

12. Kidd, *Dance of the Dissident Daughter*, 30.

13. Pittman, *Man Enough*, 253.

14. Saussy, *God Images and Self-Esteem*, 91.

15. Ntozake Shange, *for colored girls who have considered suicide when the rainbow is enuf* (New York: Macmillan, 1976), 63.

16. Kidd, *Dance of the Dissident Daughter*, 99.

17. Ibid., 42.

3. The God I Worship Does Not Want Me to Say "No"

1. Bernstein, *Female Identity Conflict*, 28–29.

2. Natalie Shainess, *Sweet Suffering: Woman as Victim* (New York: Pocket Books, 1984), 31–32.

3. Ibid., 38.

4. Rosemary Radford Ruether, *Gaia and God: An Ecofeminist Theology of Earth Healing* (San Francisco: HarperSanFrancisco, 1992), 166.

5. Luise Eichenbaum and Susie Orbach, *Understanding Women: A Feminist Psychoanalytic Approach* (New York: Basic Books, 1983), 9.

6. Arnold Cooper, "The Narcissistic-Masochistic Character," in *Masochism: Current Psychoanalytic Perspectives*, Robert A. Glick and Donald I. Meyers, eds. (Hillsdale, N.J.: The Analytic Press, 1988), 128.

4. The God I Worship Depresses Me and Denies Me Anger

1. Harriet Goldhar Lerner, *The Dance of Anger: A Woman's Guide to Changing the Patterns of Intimate Relationships* (New York: Harper & Row, 1985), 2.

2. Jean Baker Miller, *Toward a New Psychology of Women* (Boston: Beacon Press, 1976), 10.

3. David Augsburger, "Anger and Aggression," in *Clinical Handbook of Pastoral Counseling*, Robert J. Wicks, Richard D. Parsons, and Donald Capps, eds. (New York: Paulist Press, 1985), 488.

4. Lerner, *Dance of Anger*, 141.

5. Ibid., 20.

6. Ibid., 5–8.

7. Ibid., 81.

8. Augsburger, "Anger and Aggression," 487.

9. Beverly Harrison quoted in *Weaving the Visions*, 215.

10. Ibid., 217, 220.

11. Ibid., 219.

12. Ibid., 220.

13. Jeanne Stevenson Moessner, ed., *Through the Eyes of Women: Insights for Pastoral Care* (Minneapolis: Fortress Press, 1996), 115.

14. Lerner, *Dance of Anger*, 145.

15. Reilly, *A God Who Looks Like Me*, 40.

16. Sallie McFague, *Models of God: Theology for an Ecological, Nuclear Age* (Philadelphia: Fortress Press, 1987), 34.

17. Ibid., 34, 91.

18. Ibid., 106, 113.

19. Ibid., 128, 130–32.

20. Ibid., 147.

21. Ibid., 139, 162.

22. Ibid., 165.

5. The God I Worship Hurts Me

1. Mary Pellauer, Barbara Chester, and Jane Boyajian, eds., *Sexual Assault and Abuse: A Handbook for Clergy and Religious Professionals* (San Francisco: HarperSanFrancisco, 1987), 52.

2. Marie Fortune, *Sexual Violence: The Unmentionable Sin* (New York: The Pilgrim Press, 1983), 19.

3. Ibid., 20.

4. Ibid., 21, 25.

5. Ibid., 117–18.

6. Ibid., 80.

7. Ibid., 81.

8. Ibid., 82.

9. Ibid., 82–83.

10. Ibid., 87.

11. Ibid., 77.

6. Breathing New Life into Old God Images

1. Rebecca Chopp, *The Power to Speak: Feminism, Language, God* (New York: Crossroad, 1989), 111.

2. Reilly, *A God Who Looks Like Me*, 55.

7. Practical Exercises for Liberating Imaging of God for Women

1. Merlin Stone, *When God Was a Woman* (New York: Harcourt Brace Jovanovich, 1976), 10–11.